FIRST LADIES

FIRST LADIES

by

KATHLEEN PRINDIVILLE

INTRODUCTION BY ADRIENNE FOULKE

Second Edition

THE MACMILLAN COMPANY · NEW YORK
COLLIER-MACMILLAN LIMITED · LONDON

Grateful acknowledgment is given to the following for supplying photographs: Bettmann Archive: 35, 53, 70, 114, 238; Library of Congress: 22, 57, 124, 137, 143, 156, 168, 177, 179, 183, 190, 198–99, 213, 226, 229, 232, 253; Miami University, Oxford, Ohio: 207; Harry Shaw Newman, The Old Print Shop: 30–31; Smithsonian Institution: 77 (from the Adams-Clement Collection), 132 (from negative provided by Mr. Trist Wood), 151; UPI: 273, 275, 300; © Von Behr: 276; The White House: frontispiece, xii, 13, 17, 121 (Abbie Rowe); Wide World Photos: 216, 218, 246, 260, 286; Wiles-Hood Photographers: 92.

Contents

Introduction

A WOMAN fainted away when she learned that her husband had just been nominated for the American presidency. It was Jane Pierce, who was reacting with a usual, if extreme, emotion to the prospect of becoming First Lady of the land. (Sarah Polk did not faint; she merely prayed every night that her husband's opponent would win.)

If such behavior seems surprising, it is because most of us think that being a president's wife must be glamorous, exciting, utterly wonderful. It *is* the most prominent position a woman in our country can hold. It does carry with it great honor. It is always a challenge, and it can be a great opportunity. Yet most First Ladies move into the White House with regret and leave it with relief.

Thinking twice, we can begin to understand their feelings. Most women who enter the White House have never had any wish to be public figures. They have been wives and mothers, and that has mattered above all else to them. The man, it has been said, who does not want to be president can never get the job, but for his wife it is a different matter. She faces a serious conflict of interests. Loyalty and pride make her want her husband to win. When he does, affection and loyalty help her carry out her part of the job. (Sarah Polk, the one who prayed nightly, became one of the "most popular mistresses of the White House.") But she sees, too, how punishing the burdens of the presidency are, how they will weigh on her husband, even shortening his life. And if she is a mother, she faces a serious problem: how can she make it possible, with the whole world peering at their every move, for her family to live anything like normal lives?

So far, nearly forty women have had to cope with these problems. Each has had to find her own answers, because the First Lady has the additional uncertainty of finding no hard-and-fast rules to guide her. The Constitution nowhere mentions such a job as hers; no later law has ever established it; no one, including her predecessors, has ever defined it. When she moves into the White House she is, to an amazing degree, on her own—and this in the fullest public view.

Rules, no, but certain patterns of conduct, yes. Perhaps more than any other American institution, the job of being First Lady is a matter of tradition. Over almost two hundred years, a handful of women have, by their personalities and performances, created that tradition. They could scarcely have been more varied. They have been young and old, beautiful and plain, stylish and dowdy. Some have been outgoing, others painfully shy; some socially accomplished, others awkward. A number have been widely educated and traveled, while others have not had these advantages. A few have been definitely interested in politics and public affairs, whereas others have hardly known the names of the men in their husbands' cabinets. All these women have contributed something, nonetheless, to our image of the American First Lady. And the very fact that they have included such a range of personalities has given the role a precious flexibility that allows each woman to adjust to her official situation in her own best way.

Martha Custis Washington, as the first First Lady, limited her public activity to that of hostess. All her successors have considered this their primary official duty. When the First Lady entertains in her "home," at great formal dinners and receptions, she realizes that she is acting not only for herself and the President, but for the American people. She must meet strangers by the thousands with friendliness and grace. There have been great hostesses in the White House, from Dolley Madison to Jacqueline Kennedy, whose elegance and flair have been a genuine asset to their President-husbands—and have delighted the country as well, for the public loves a truly good show.

At the same time, the American people have been surprisingly respectful—given our tendency to think that public figures are common property—when a First Lady has preferred to live in as inconspicuous and retiring a way as possible. Many have chosen to do so. Poor health has occasionally made the President's wife a virtual recluse, as with Ida McKinley. A reserved nature, as in the case of Mamie Eisenhower, may make them shun public attention. These women have kept largely to the second-floor apartments of the White House, the one place where a First Family can live in privacy, and where no one goes except by personal invitation.

A different temperament or ability and a different kind of working relationship with their husbands have, on the other hand, produced some very active and politically influential First Ladies. Abigail Fillmore worked as her husband's private secretary, and shared in his political decisions as President. Helen Taft was actually responsible for her husband's nomination. Howard Taft would have preferred to serve on the Supreme Court but agreed to run, saying with philosophical wryness that, since "my wife is the politician, and she will be able to meet all . . . issues, perhaps we can keep a stiff upper lip." Important as she was during her husband's administration, Mrs. Taft was careful to remain in the background. Only some ten years later, Edith Wilson could not do that. She largely took over during the long months when Woodrow Wilson was too ill to carry out his duties. It is true that Mrs. Wilson worked closely with her husband and always acted in his name, but it was really she who made official appointments and took decisions in what some have called "Mrs. Wilson's Regency."

It was Eleanor Roosevelt, however, who, with no wish to be a substitute president, greatly expanded the activities of the First Lady. A combination of factors explains why she functioned in a more active, and in a more openly and politically effective, way than any president's wife before or since. She had a warm, unflagging interest in people of all kinds; she held strong and often unorthodox opinions about almost everything except food; she knew how to channel a truly formidable energy; since her husband could not move about freely, he relied on her being "his eyes"; last but not least, she responded to the fact that the role of women in modern society was changing and growing. Very likely, no one quite like her will ever follow, but, by what she was and what she did, Eleanor Roosevelt enormously enlarged the public's idea of what a First Lady can potentially be.

What kind of wife and mother a First Lady is will remain a private matter. But it is now obvious that the nineteenth century role of official hostess is only one part of a First Lady's public significance. The combined effect of all our public communications—television, radio, newsreels, magazines, and press—highlights the performance of any First Lady and makes her a force in modern American life.

She herself may have no strong political interests, but she is now so much in the public eye, at home and abroad, that she must have political *sense*; that is, at the very least, she must learn to avoid even the seemingly trivial slips that can have embarrassing consequences. There is the more positive side. Her own interests and tastes actually help to form and develop the interests and tastes of millions of people. This is true not merely in matters of fashion or personal style, although here public response, especially from women, is very noticeable. Just as the President now acts not only on the national but on the international scene, so the First Lady is now powerfully present in the American home. Every person in the country is very much aware of her particular qualities and accomplishments. People tend to respond to all that she shows she values and appreciates, with fresh interest and regard. She can provide immense stimulus and encouragement in many areas of life, from social service to sports and the arts.

Certainly, future First Ladies will continue to feel that their first responsibility is to husband and family. To the extent that they do play a public role, it will be a supporting one. But they will all realize that it is within their power, as never before, to be a creative influence in the social and cultural life of the nation.

—ADRIENNE FOULKE

Jacqueline Bouvier Kennedy

(1929)

"What kind of person is she? What's she really like?" The reporters milled around, pressing questions on her, but Letitia Baldridge, holding her first press conference as social secretary to the new First Lady, was unruffled. "Jacqueline Kennedy," she said, "is the young woman who has everything—including the President of the United States."

The press people laughed and tried again. Jacqueline Kennedy was no stranger to them. She had lived in Washington for seven years as the wife of a very active and prominent Senator. She had shared in the recent presidential campaign in which the nation—upsetting many predictions —chose its first Catholic family for the White House. And now this immensely attractive woman was, at thirty-one, soon to become First Lady. What she did, said, thought— what she didn't do, think, or say—was news. But as one of the reporters remarked, the woman herself was "a puzzlement." She didn't fit any of the formulas. Hers was no rags to riches story; not a work-to-win story. It was not even a too-good-to-be-true story, for it was all true!

Fortune favored Jacqueline Bouvier from the very first.

She was born July 28, 1929, the year of the Great Depression, but her parents happened to be not only young and attractive but wealthy. As a child, her homes were a large apartment in New York and a house in the charming Long Island village of Southampton, with its spreading fields and great beaches. Her childhood problem was not how to do without advantages, but rather to learn how to make the most of all of them. In brief, she was born into what is called—sometimes with an uneasy note of apology—American aristocracy. The obligations this puts on a child are several; for example, a child will learn French while he is still mastering English; he will learn to ride while he is still learning to walk. The little Bouvier girl was placed on a pony's back before she was a year old.

Indeed, animals played an important part in Jackie's young life. The little girl shared her bedroom—or so she regularly informed her family—with a brown bear. It is a fact that her father allowed her to keep a rabbit in the bathtub of their New York apartment. Her Caprice (a Belgian dog looking rather like a schnauzer) figured as the heroine in a series of stories Jackie wrote and illustrated herself. Her view of her own future she spelled out in another romance of which she was the heroine—the circus queen who marries the man on the flying trapeze.

In the world of grownups, Jackie was sturdily—her mother says fiercely—independent. It seems quite believable that if such a child found herself (as Jackie did) alone in Central Park when she was only four, she would march up to a policeman, give him her home telephone to call—and, when her mother arrived, announced that it was not she but her nurse who had gotten lost. There is some connection between such self-reliance and the fact that by five

Jackie was already a promising horsewoman. A lifelong passion for riding was already well rooted.

The little girl was busy with more than horses, however. Both she and her sister Lee, three and a half years younger, were keenly intelligent. Mrs. Bouvier taught Jackie to read long before she went to school, and by the time she was six she had already read by herself such favorites as *Winnie the Pooh* and *The Wizard of Oz*. This appetite for reading has never flagged, and it is one she shares today with her husband. (When they first knew each other, he was quite as likely to send her a book on history or politics as a bouquet of flowers.) Like all voracious readers, Jacqueline reads anywhere, anytime. Once, while campaigning with the Senator in Wisconsin, she was noticed in a rear car of the motorcade, absorbed in the second volume of General de Gaulle's memoirs.

School proved to be an unwelcome confinement. At Miss Chapin's, an exclusive school in New York City, Jacqueline was restive. She hated having to wear a school uniform (as she says, "I've always loved clothes") and she was otherwise mildly rebellious, with the result that although always a good student, she performed less well academically than she could have. Matters went somewhat more smoothly at Miss Porter's, a private boarding school in Connecticut for wealthy young girls. This is not to say that Jackie had become a conformist. The thumbnail sketch accompanying her photograph in the 1947 classbook suggests two aspects, a typical and a far-from-typical teen-ager:

> Jacqueline Lee Bouvier
> "Merrywood" McLean, Virginia
> "Jackie"

Favorite song:	Lime House Blues
Always saying:	"Play a rhumba next."
Most known for:	Wit
Aversion:	People who ask if her horse is still alive
Where found:	Laughing with Tucky
Ambition:	Not to be a housewife

Not to be a housewife! To this day, Jacqueline Bouvier Kennedy, who is acclaimed one of the greatest hostesses the White House has ever had, cannot cook and cannot sew. "She simply isn't interested in that sort of thing," a sister-in-law has said. She is a devoted wife and mother, and a fiercely protective homemaker. She can plan a menu with the skill of a professional (she does plan all her menus), but stops there. Her mother, now Mrs. Auchincloss,* confirms that this was always so. When her daughter launched her project of restoring the interior of the White House, Mrs. Auchincloss said with equal parts of admiration and surprise: "As a young girl she was never even interested in selecting a chair for a room. She was a real scholar, and the world of books and the arts mattered most to her."

Those were the things that absorbed young Jacqueline Bouvier at Vassar, where for her first two years she was an A student. Weekends were not slighted, however, and her father commented glumly on how many young men made a weekly pilgrimage up the Hudson: he was anxious that she should not marry too young. On off-campus weekends, if she was not going home, she went to Harvard or Yale or Princeton. She herself says of this period: "I really did enjoy the parties and dances. But Newport—when I was about nineteen, I knew I didn't want the rest of my life to

* The Bouviers were divorced when Jacqueline was a young girl, and her mother remarried.

be there. I didn't want to marry any of the young men I grew up with—not because of them but because of their life. I didn't know what I wanted. I was still floundering."

In this restless, half-searching mood, she got permission to join a Smith College group going to study in France for the junior year. It proved to be a great and important year in her life. She lived in a cultivated French home; she studied at the Sorbonne, where students are completely on their own but must meet impeccable standards of work. She developed her French to a native's fluency. (French had been spoken at table at home in New York. "We had twelve matches each, and anybody who let slip an English word paid a match.") She read, worked at the Art Institute, got into long discussions with very bright, very serious young university men, traveled a bit about Europe—and all these were steps away from "floundering" in Newport. "I had the most terrific vacation in Austria and Germany," she wrote her stepbrother Hugh Auchincloss. "We saw Vienna and Salzburg and Berchtesgaden, where Hitler lived. . . . It's so much more fun traveling second and third class and sitting up all night in trains, as you really get to know people —and hear their stories. When I traveled before it was all too luxurious, and we didn't see anything."

Back in the United States and a senior at George Washington University, Jacqueline opened a note one day from her mother, in which Mrs. Auchincloss enclosed an announcement of *Vogue's* annual Prix de Paris competition. It was open to women college seniors, and she urged Jacqueline to try her hand at it. Now, this contest is no sleazy publicity stunt. Each contestant must submit four papers on fashion subjects, a description of herself, a plan for an entire issue of the magazine, and a five-hundred-word essay on "People I Wish I Had Known." As her "people," Jacqueline chose Baudelaire, Diaghilev, and Oscar Wilde. The first prize traditionally includes six months' work abroad on the staff of the Paris edition. That year there were 1,280 contestants from two hundred and twenty-five accredited colleges. The first prize was awarded to Jacqueline Bouvier, but she, after a sharp struggle, declined it. "I guess I was too scared to go," she explained later. "I felt then that if I went back I'd live there forever, because I loved Paris so much. It's such a formative year, don't you think, the first one after you get out of college?"

She had made a more influential decision than she could have known at the time. Had she gone back to Paris, the whole course of her life would certainly have been different. But what was she to do with that "formative" year? She did not need to earn her living, of course, but she was trained—and she was still "fiercely independent." She was interested in writing, and throughout her school life had worked on school papers. She could be a reporter, perhaps? Jacqueline was living at the time with her mother, stepfather, and their combined large family on a charming country property near Washington, so the capital seemed the obvious place to look for work. Newspaper jobs are not easily come by there, and Jackie was becoming discouraged when the editor of the *Times-Herald* told her the Inquiring Camera Girl spot was open. It was a junior reporter's job. It involved thinking up questions—sometimes serious, sometimes for a laugh—then persuading people on the street to answer, taking a good picture of each, and writing up the column. How was she with a camera, by the way? Oh, the applicant said vaguely, she could handle one pretty well. (And so she could—a Brownie!) "You never saw a girl from a family of multimillionaires so tickled to get a $42.50 a week job," a newspaper colleague said later. Jacqueline took a rush camera course at a school she found through the classified telephone book. That helped, but her real salvation came from the ace photographer on the *Herald*. "He stretched himself on the floor to measure six feet," she recalls, "and told me to take all my pictures from that distance."

Jacqueline worked a year and a half on the *Herald*, and she must have done a decent job. She got a raise (she was earning $56.75 when she left), more than once she got her column on the front page, and the *Herald* sent her to London to cover the Coronation of Elizabeth II. In the light of later events, two of her interviews have a certain interest. After the election of Mr. Eisenhower, in 1952, camera-reporter Bouvier stationed herself outside the school attended by two nieces of Mrs. Eisenhower, aged ten and eleven. Snagging them as they came out, she asked how it felt to be the nieces of the President. Their rather naïve answers, plus the photographs and sketches she added, made the kind of "human-interest" story all city editors love, but if the incident is ever recalled by the present Jacqueline Kennedy as she wages the battle for her children's privacy that all White House mothers must fight, she probably feels rather rueful. Another assignment that now has its droll side came when her boss sent her out to interview that popular bachelor and man-about-town, young Senator John Kennedy. "But don't get your hopes up," the city editor warned her as she was leaving.

Actually, the young couple had already met the summer before at the home of mutual friends, spent a pleasant evening, and gone their separate ways. Now, some seven months later, the interview was quickly followed by their going dancing at the Shoreham Hotel. This was their one public date. They saw each other after that only alone or with friends—perhaps going to a movie—but even this was infrequent. John Kennedy was often out of town, fighting hard for the senatorship from Massachusetts. He flew down to see Jacqueline whenever he could. "He'd call me from some oyster bar up there, with a great clinking of coins, to ask me out to the movies the following Wednesday," she remembers. It surely never occurred to her how typical this hectic, scrambled pattern would become for them both.

Kennedy saw her off to London, however, on her Coronation assignment, and while she was in Europe she received a few short cables from him. A sample: "Articles excellent but you are missed." Although Jacqueline once confided to a newspaper friend that "What I wanted more than anything in the world was to be married to him," both young people exhibited a very agreeable reticence in public about their feelings for each other. And so it was that, on her return, Jacqueline quietly resigned from the *Times-Herald* and, allowing *Look* magazine just time enough to banner an article on Washington's Most Eligible Young Bachelor, they announced their engagement on June 25, 1953. She was twenty-three and he, thirty-six.

A fabulous wedding, a short honeymoon in Mexico, and the young couple were back in Washington where Mrs. Kennedy began to organize her life as a senator's wife. Organization was called for. Their pattern was still relatively simple, but it demanded considerable entertaining, which could—and often did—start with breakfast. On one occasion it involved forty guests for lunch, which was a challenge to the hostess, chiefly because the Senator forgot to mention having invited them until an hour before they were to arrive. "I was always prepared for eight," she said mildly, once the crisis was behind her.

Heavy troubles, however, hung over their young marriage. The Senator's back, hurt while he was playing football at Harvard, and further damaged during the wreck of his PT boat in World War II, steadily worsened until, in desperation, he gambled on a very dangerous operation. He nearly lost the gamble, and Jacqueline her husband, but finally he began to mend. He faced a long, painful convalescence—months in bed, and later, almost a year on crutches. During this hard pull, Jacqueline Kennedy was with him every day. She read to him; she brought him special food; sometimes she just sat quietly in the room for company. When he started to improve and set to work on *Profiles in Courage,* which won the Pulitzer Prize, she did research for the book. The Senator expressed what this meant to him in dedicating the work to her: "This book would not have been possible without the encouragement, assistance and criticisms offered from the very beginning by my wife Jacqueline, whose help during all the days of my convalescence I cannot ever adequately acknowledge."

The next year, it was she who had to fight for health after the bitter disappointment of the loss of their first baby. Enormously unlike as they are in temperament, John and Jacqueline Kennedy are alike in this: neither gives up when fighting for something he believes is important. By 1956, needing his crutches only occasionally, the Senator was back in the political arena, working vigorously this time to win the Democratic vice-presidential nomination. And Jacqueline, who has said so often how she longs for a large family, was again expecting a child. Her doctors forbade any unusual exertion. During those grueling preconvention months she saw her husband seldom, and she suffered acutely from the sense that, of all the Kennedy clan, she was the only one unable to help his candidacy in any active way. His defeat by Senator Estes Kefauver—a blessing in disguise, as it later turned out—left Kennedy exhausted and frustrated, and he took off alone for a rest at his parents' house in southern France. He was at sea on the family yacht when his wife was prematurely confined and her child delivered stillborn. By the time he did receive word, her life was hanging in the balance. Racing home, he found that he could in return offer her the support and companionship that helps turn the tide of illness back toward health.

Friends describe Jacqueline Kennedy in various ways. They need scarcely point out that she is lovely to look at; that she has a far more rare thing, a personal style; and that she dresses with taste and flair. She is, they say, warm and friendly but—someone always adds—she *is* shy; she is the kind of person who needs some privacy, some time to herself in which to think or just be alone. Marriage to a man with the drive of John Kennedy—a man who was clearly on the rise in national affairs—such a marriage for such a woman must have called for great adjustments. "I married a whirlwind," she said once. "He's indestructible. People who try to keep up with him drop like flies." She did not drop like a fly. She adjusted. Indeed, they both did.

That fall and winter of 1956 was a period of restored health and relative calm, a period for consolidating a still very new marriage that had been subjected to severe strains. Neither John nor Jacqueline supposed that it would be more than a short respite between political campaigns, in which they would have the leisure to go about together and to enjoy each other. She learned to play golf and to water-ski, and they were seen together at the theater or in art galleries. They found fresh areas of interest to share through books. "We both have inquiring minds," Mrs. Kennedy once said. "That's the reason we chose each other. I have always felt so alive with him."

For the Kennedys, a peak of happiness was reached with the birth, in 1957, of a solid, sturdy daughter, Caroline Lee. By the time the 1958 congressional election came round, Mrs. Kennedy was able to play a far more active part. She toured Massachusetts with her husband, and little by little acquired the knack of how to be a politician's wife. When her husband's huge senatorial majority was tallied, his wife could have the satisfaction of knowing that she had contributed toward it.

The next time round was, of course, the big time. It came only two years later, in 1960. During Kennedy's campaign for the presidency, Jacqueline Kennedy was again expecting a child and again under firm instructions from her doctors to be very quiet. For all that, she managed to be an amazingly effective member of her husband's team. During the primaries, she campaigned with him from time to time, and during the critical Wisconsin primary, when he had suddenly to fly back to Washington, she briefly took over and made personal appearances for him. Her style was anything but orthodox. "We've been working so hard in Wisconsin," she told one luncheon meeting, "and I know that if you see fit to support my husband you will find you haven't misplaced your trust." Compared to the usual high-pressured electioneering talk, this sounds a bit flat, but people responded to her simplicity and directness. She was so clearly not competitive or ambitious for herself: "Jack wouldn't—couldn't—have a wife who shared the spotlight with him," she explained once. "And I think that a wife's happiness comes in what makes her husband happy."

She wisely avoided the hurly-burly of the convention, but found some ingenious and utterly characteristic ways to support her candidate-husband in the campaign that followed. She gave teas for prominent women Democrats; she wrote a chatty syndicated weekly column called "Campaign Wife"; during the decisive TV debates between Senator Kennedy and Mr. Nixon, she instituted the Television Listening Parties; she wrote letters and organized the Calling for Kennedy Drive; she posed for photographs, appeared with her husband on TV specials. Her boost to Kennedy's plurality in the big cities, whose votes were essential to his success, was most helpful. When, as on Columbus Day in New York, she faced a large Puerto Rican rally and began simply *"Buenos días, mis amigos,"* she added a powerful campaign appeal. Jacqueline's friendly and forthright little speeches in Spanish, Italian, and French before foreign-speaking audiences and over the radio had tremendous impact. They foreshadowed, too, the warm response she would win for herself and her country when, as First Lady, she traveled to Latin America and Europe, and could speak with pleasant fluency her hosts' native languages.

In her first days as a Senator's wife, newsmen had commented on Mrs. Kennedy's prompt and courteous handling of reasonable questions. She understood about press deadlines, too. With time, she had added adroitness in parrying the more tricky questions and doing it without any loss of her characteristic directness. In the last days of the campaign—they were in her own word "unbearable"—she was

asked what the family's plans were for after election day. She smiled and said simply, "We have two different sets of plans." She bore the strain to the very end, and rode with her husband through a New York ticker-tape parade only two weeks before election day. People generally agreed that it had been a thoroughbred's performance from a woman whose second child—John F. Kennedy, Jr.—was born only two weeks and two days after her husband's election to the presidency.

Before the Kennedys moved into the White House, Jacqueline Kennedy had replied to a reporter: "I'll be a wife and mother first, then First Lady." Like Frances Cleveland, who also had very young children in the White House, Mrs. Kennedy soon found that privacy for the First Family required having a home away from home. In addition to their personal quarters on the second floor of the White House, they can now go to the eight-room white clapboard house in Hyannis Port. Closer at hand is a weekend house in Atoka, Virginia.

The time Mrs. Kennedy spends in the country is one target for her critics. Like all public figures, the President's wife gets her share, and perhaps more, of negative comment. However, Mrs. Kennedy feels that the weekends at the Virginia house are important for her family. The property is secluded, which is ideal for them; the rolling countryside is perfect for the riding she enjoys and is teaching to her children. In short, it is here that they can relax in relative seclusion and truly be together as a family.

Notwithstanding the critics, she has, so far, achieved this degree of privacy without the smallest apparent neglect of her official duties as President's wife. Indeed, Jacqueline Kennedy was quickly praised as one of the greatest of White House hostesses. People who enjoy historical comparisons liken her to Dolley Madison, while others are content to admire a gracious and tasteful performance. The key to the success of both women is probably a matter of attitude. As Mrs. Kennedy has said, managing a house and entertaining are "a joy to me. . . . When it all runs smoothly, when the food is good . . . the flowers look fresh . . . I have such satisfaction."

But the success begins with the preparations, of which she herself takes care. She plans the menus, for small dinners, usually not more than four courses; selects and arranges the flowers in simple wicker baskets—generally, seasonal garden flowers like daisies, larkspur, freesia, tulips—that combine charmingly with pastel table linens. The guests? "Being in the White House does make friendships difficult. Nobody

feels the same. Jack's even more isolated than I, so I do try
to have a few friends for dinner as often as possible . . .
someone we know really well, because I hate to call and
have people feel they have to come."

In more formal entertaining, the impress of the First
Lady's tastes is just as evident. Manners are more relaxed;
if there must be a receiving line, the Kennedys presently
leave it and circulate freely among their guests. More significantly, the habitual list of diplomats, government big-
wigs, and business leaders has been expanded to include a
genuine cross section of public figures. The great innovation is the number of people concerned with the arts—poets,
painters, architects, actors, musicians—who are now invited
to White House ceremonies. Obviously, this reflects Mrs.
Kennedy's—and also the President's—personal interests,
and it has had a stimulating effect on public attitudes toward the arts.

These same interests undoubtedly underlie the most sub-
stantial contribution Jacqueline Kennedy has made to public life in her first years as First Lady—the restoration of the
interior of the White House.

Others had attempted a similar if less ambitious project,
and she was careful to learn from their difficulties. Charac-
teristically, she had no wish to impose her personal tastes.
As she put it, "I don't have a [basic plan] because I think
this house will always grow and should. It just seemed to
me such a shame when we came here to find hardly anything of the past in the house, hardly anything before
1902." She had seen the presidential palace in Colombia,
and noticed that every piece of furniture had some link with
the past. "I thought the White House should be like that."
She gathered together a committee of museum experts, and

government and private authorities on art history, to share in deciding what should be discarded and what added. To avoid all-too-familiar money difficulties with Congress, she arranged for all new accessions to come as gifts, and, while the job has not been done with schoolchildren's pennies, this has made for a basis of public participation.

In February 1962, more than one third of the nation watched a television show in which Mrs. Kennedy gave a personally conducted tour of the renovated rooms. Emil Ludwig once wrote that the White House is "not splendid enough for a castle but more striking than a private home. The patrician aspect of this house is at once almost princely and yet private. One would say that here lives a father of a country." To the TV audience that night it was clear that an expert job had been done in just that spirit to make a reality of Mrs. Kennedy's conviction that "everything in the White House should be the best."

Mrs. Kennedy's other tours have taken her away from the White House—to Canada and Latin America, to India and Pakistan, to England, Austria, and France, Italy and Greece. Some have been visits of state made with her husband, who once acknowledged the wildly enthusiastic welcome she was given, saying "I'm the man who accompanied Jackie Kennedy to Paris." Some were so-called private trips that have brought her into contact with fascinating world figures. Again and again her unaffected ways, which captivate people quite as much as her most artfully groomed appearance, are reflected in her own comments. When told she had had an unusually long time alone with Pope John, she said, "He's such a good man—so of the earth, and centuries of kindness in his eyes. . . . [The audience] didn't seem long. It was all so simple and natural. We didn't talk

of anything serious. . . ." Explaining her astrakhan hat, the gift of President Ayub Khan of Pakistan, she said, "I asked to try his, and it was just right, and so he gave it to me." Wherever she goes the reporters are there, too, and every word, every move, is recorded in minute detail, later to appear in papers all over the world. An individual can learn, with time, to take this kind of ceaseless pressure, but Jacqueline Kennedy has not been changed by having become a public image. As she flew back home from her last trip abroad, it was a wife, not the First Lady, speaking, when she said to a friend, "I just pray I was all right and that the trip did some good. . . . Jack's always so proud of me when I do something like this, but I can't stand being out in front. I know it sounds trite, but what I really want is to be behind him and to be a good wife and mother."

Now that we have seen how a contemporary First Lady handles the duties and obligations confronting her, let us review the performances of women who carried out this demanding role in the past.

Most of them were wives of presidents, but sometimes the burden fell to a daughter, a daughter-in-law, or a niece. Each succeeded in varying degrees and by different methods, according to her temperament. Some were publicly more active than others, and some assumed a larger part than others in the work of the president and his career. Martha Washington, the first First Lady, initiated this honorable tradition.

Martha (Dandridge) Custis Washington
(1732–1802)

ONE crisp morning in the autumn of 1761, a young woman rode across the Virginia fields. She laughed as the wind tried to snatch her soft plumed hat—she was happy to be riding at the side of her soldierly husband, happy to be mistress of the plantation home to which he had recently brought her.

As she put her horse over ditches and gave him his head on clear stretches, she felt no presentiment that those days in the mellow Virginia countryside could end. Except for a season or two at the viceregal court in Williamsburg, Martha had known nothing but green pines, wide fields bright with yellowing tobacco, white mansions set back in swept plantation yards. As the eldest child of Colonel John Dandridge and Frances Jones Dandridge, she had grown to girlhood at her birthplace, the large plantation on the Pamunkey River.

Until she was fifteen, her days were filled by lessons in sewing, housekeeping, cooking, dancing, and music. She was called not long after the slaves were awakened by their work horn; her day began at six, with a lesson in reading and writing in the study room, where the Dandridge tutor awaited her with a hornbook, copybook and goose-quill pen. While she studied aloud, he sat by the fire and mended a pen or two with his knife, or dissolved ink powders into writing fluid. He seemed to pay no attention to his young scholar; but the moment her voice dropped he recalled her attention to study: "Come now, Mistress Patsy, you must spell the words aloud. How am I to know that you are applying yourself if I do not hear you study?"

Just before breakfast, there was half an hour of bothersome ciphers, the half-hour when Martha scratched dismally at "reductions ascending" and "reductions descending" and wished she could scrunch the numbers between her fingers like eggs. It was hard, after that painful work, not to race to breakfast the moment she heard the bell; but she had been schooled to rise slowly from her bench, drop a curtsy to her tutor, then walk gravely into the dining room, where she curtsied again before taking her place.

Until dinnertime at midafternoon she practiced sewing, knitting, spinning, weaving, cooking. During all the hours that she hemmed and cross-stitched, overseamed and looped, she sat very straight and still on an uncushioned stool, her back stiffly supported by pack thread stays, her feet—demurely square to the floor in their high-heeled satin slippers —scarcely showing beneath the edge of her hooped gown. She also worked hard in the hours between dinner and supper. Her only lessons then were in dancing and at the spinet, but her master was equally earnest in teaching her how to curtsy, to take a gentleman's hand and step in the country dances and rigadoons, as he was in teaching her how to read.

She had learned her lessons and graces well by the time she was fifteen, when Colonel and Mrs. Dandridge prepared to present her at the viceregal court in Williamsburg. The little Virginia town was then a center of Colonial fashion and a miniature of the court of King George II, ruler of America. Williamsburg society carried itself with a very grand air, its ladies and gentlemen dressing in the latest modes from France and England; so Colonel Dandridge sent abroad for Martha's court attire. When a stout sailing vessel tied up at Annapolis after its long ocean voyage, there were in its hold lengths of glossy velvet and satin, ruffles and tuckers and gloves, fans and slender slippers for Mistress Martha Dandridge. Just as soon as they arrived at the plantation on the Pamunkey, the sewing room began to hum, and Martha helped to fashion the velvet into sacques, the satin into ball gowns.

At the opening of the court season she was driven into Williamsburg, her great four-horse coach sinking almost hub deep in the sandy streets, which were laid out in the form of a W and an M, in honor of William and Mary. Then, at gay routs, bewigged officers on the staff of His Majesty's Governor—gallant in brocade coats and silken breeches—acclaimed her vivacity and brown-haired beauty. There at court, too, Colonel Daniel Parke Custis bowed over her hand, and paid suit to her.

Although Colonel Custis was several years her senior, Martha accepted him, and they were married in 1749, making their home at the White House on York River, Virginia, and at Six Chimneys House in Williamsburg. Of their four children, two died in childhood, and only John Parke Custis and Martha Parke Custis lived to survive their father, who died in 1757.

A year after the death of her husband, the Widow Custis went to visit at the nearby estate of Major Chamberlayne.

One May morning, not long after her arrival there, a tall young soldier of Virginia rode to a ferry at the foot of the plantation. It was Colonel George Washington, lately returned from the tragic Braddock campaign, and with him was his body servant, Bishop. Catching sight of the young Virginian, Major Chamberlayne hurried to meet him, and invited him to rest at Chamberlayne House.

He could not stay a moment, Colonel Washington declared. Thoroughly engrossed in the business at hand, he explained that he was hurrying to Williamsburg on official matters. Major Chamberlayne increased the attraction of his invitation by adding that "charming Madam Custis" was his guest. Colonel Washington hesitated a moment, and then decided that his business in Williamsburg could wait until he had at least gallantly met and paid his respects to the young widow.

Colonel Washington did not ride to Williamsburg that day, nor did he leave Chamberlayne House until late next morning, for he had found Madam Custis quite as charming as the Major had promised.

On his way back from Williamsburg, Colonel Washington stopped to see Martha again, this time, at the Custis White House to which she had returned, and before he left for the Ohio campaign they were engaged. At the end of the wilderness expedition in January of 1759, he hurried back to her for their marriage. He had resigned his commission in His Majesty's army, and so laid aside his field uniform for a wedding suit of blue cloth, with a coat lined in red silk and trimmed in silver and an embroidered white satin waistcoat. His shoe and knee buckles were of gold, and a dress sword hung at his side.

In her wedding dress, Martha Custis looked very young,

very much like the girl who had been belle of the Williams-burg court. Her quilted petticoat was of white satin, and over it she wore a heavy corded white silk skirt with point lace and ruffles. On her white satin slippers were diamond buckles. Her necklace, earrings, and bracelet were of pearls, and in her hair were pearl ornaments.

After the ceremony Colonel Washington handed her into her chariot. Then, mounting his own horse, he accompanied her—with an escort of former brother officers in His Majesty's service—to the White House on the York, where they made their home for several months before going to Mount Vernon.

Once the affairs of the White House estate were settled, Colonel Washington took his wife and her two children to Mount Vernon, his own plantation, from which he wrote to a kinsman in England: "I am now, I believe, fixed in this spot with an agreeable partner for life; and I hope to find more happiness in retirement than I ever experienced in the wide and bustling world."

For a few years nothing threatened this quiet life of George Washington, planter, and Martha Washington, mistress of Mount Vernon. Their hospitality was famous throughout Virginia—so famous that they were seldom alone—and the Colonel felt prompted to write in his diary: "Would anyone believe that with 101 cows . . . I should still be obliged to buy butter for my family?"

The master of Mount Vernon was an ardent huntsman —although not a good one, as he often admitted regretfully in his journal—and during the fox season his home was an open house to hunting parties. Frequently, Martha rode over the countryside with the Colonel and his guests; but more often she spent the autumn days at home, arranging savory dinners for riders who would return hungry and chilled.

But not all the guests came just to ride and dine with Colonel Washington and his lady. There were others— young Patrick Henry, Edmund Pendleton, Richard Henry Lee, and George Mason, author of the Bill of Rights. They knew their host as leader in the Virginia House of Burgesses, a man with whom they could discuss the affairs of the harassed Colonies and the laws which England was forcing upon them. But there came a lull in the stormy talk of freedom, and it seemed as though, after all, the pleasant plantation days would go on without end.

There were to be breaks in Martha's happiness, however; first was the death of her daughter, Martha Parke Custis, in 1773. When her son John was married a year later to Eleanor Calvert, Martha was still too grief-stricken to attend the wedding. Instead, she wrote to Eleanor:

My dear Nelly—God took from Me a Daughter when June roses were blooming. He has given me another daughter about her age when Winter winds are blowing, to warm my Heart again. . . . Pray receive my Benediction and a wish that you may long live the Loving Wife of my happy Son, and a Loving Daughter.

Your Affectionate Mother,
M. WASHINGTON.

Just a few months later came the second break, in September of 1774, although neither Martha nor Washington then realized its full importance. Boston had held its celebrated Tea Party; England had retaliated by closing the port of Boston, and the outraged colonists had organized a General Congress to decide what they should do. With

Patrick Henry and Pendleton, Colonel Washington set out to attend the Congress in Philadelphia. As she watched the three determined patriots ride off to do their part in securing justice for the Colonies, Martha called to them: "I hope that you will stand firm—I know that George will." Then she went back into the house and wrote to a kinswoman: "My mind is made up. My heart is in the cause." She, too, declared herself a supporter of the struggling Colonies.

Nor did she change her mind in the turbulent year that followed. Her heart was still in the cause when, in June of 1775, she learned that her husband had been chosen to lead the American troops. The war, with all its hardships and tragedy, was to become of personal concern to her.

From Philadelphia, where he was attending the Second Congress, Washington wrote to her: "I now sit down to write you on a subject which fills me with inexpressible concern. . . . You may believe me, my dear Patsy, when I assure you in the most solemn manner that, so far from seeking this appointment, I have used every endeavor in my power to avoid it. . . . I shall feel no pain from the toil or danger of the campaign; my unhappiness will flow from the uneasiness you will feel from being left alone. I therefore beg that you will summon your whole fortitude, and pass your time as agreeably as possible."

To stay at home and pass the time as agreeably as possible was not, however, Martha's idea. She at once wrote for permission to join him; and he at first refused, thinking that she would be safer in Virginia. By autumn he admitted that he needed her companionship. Immediately, she set out in her coach and four, journeying to his Cambridge headquarters.

When she arrived there in December, 1775, Martha

found that she could help him in an unexpected way. Washington was troubled by the petty jealousies of his hastily organized staff. Military affairs like the siege of Boston had perplexed him less. The staff situation called for the tact and charm of a friendly woman, and Martha was such a woman. She quickly brought harmony to Washington's headquarters by making the officers' wives, and the officers themselves, her friends.

After he had forced General Howe to evacuate Boston, Washington moved the American headquarters to New York, and Martha returned to Mount Vernon. She remained there through the disheartening months that brought the American defeats at Long Island and Harlem Heights, and the flight of the Continental troops across New Jersey—losses which were followed by Washington's brilliant victory at Trenton on Christmas Eve, when he routed the Hessians.

Home at Mount Vernon she knitted and sewed, and in the plantation workroom sixteen spinning wheels steadily turned out material for a ragged Continental army. She worked from dawn until nightfall, yet felt that she was not doing enough. She would have been at her husband's side, except that he forbade it; but when he fell sick at his Morristown headquarters, she journeyed once more to a winter encampment, arriving there in March, 1777. Camp supplies were low, the soldiers discouraged. They seldom had enough to eat or wear, and their struggle against England seemed a hopeless one. As soon as Martha had nursed her husband back to health, she at once set to cheering the forlorn camp. She visited the soldiers, and banded the officers' wives into sewing groups to make clothes for the needy troops. The tattered soldiers responded to her kindliness, soon recapturing some of the faith with which they had begun the fight for liberty.

Not long after her arrival in camp, a group of Morristown women called upon her, but they did not find the "grand lady" they had expected. One of them, Mrs. Troupe, afterwards described the visit: "We dressed ourselves in our most elegant ruffles and silks, and were introduced to her ladyship . . . we found her knitting and with a specked apron on! . . . There we were without a stitch of work and sitting in State, but General Washington's lady was knitting stockings. . . ."

When Martha returned to Mount Vernon for the summer, she again made the workroom hum; but when the winter of 1778 arrived, bringing the tragic encampment of Valley Forge, she once more took her place at headquarters. All through that cheerless winter she carried baskets of food to the sick, trudged into the miserable camp to encourage the veterans, and returned to her own cramped quarters in the Potts' house to knit and patch and make coats for them.

Every year she joined General Washington at winter headquarters, and every year the soldiers found their hardships more endurable because she was in camp. Not until the final encampment of 1783 did she leave them, and then —almost two years after the surrender of General Cornwallis at Yorktown—their "Lady Washington" said goodbye and returned to Mount Vernon. She had spent eight winters in camp life and had, as she often told her grandchildren later, heard the opening and closing shot of almost every important campaign in the Revolution.

When she and General Washington returned to Mount Vernon on Christmas Eve, at the close of the war, it seemed as though she had ended her service to her country. She wanted only the homely life of the plantation, but General Washington had become too great a leader in American life to slip back into the routine of a Virginia farmer. The nation summoned him to the presidency, and so Martha prepared to leave Mount Vernon again, to go to the Executive Mansion in New York.

She was fifty-seven years old—and tired. She had almost forgotten that she had queened it in Williamsburg society in the courtly days of English rule; but, without a pause, she set about her work as the First Lady of the Land. There was no precedent to guide her. She had to be the model for all who would succeed her in the Executive Mansion. Directed by her own good sense and social training, she deftly established the duties of her position. Each Friday night she held a levee, with President Washington at her side, greeting all who came to pay their respects. Formal attire was required of those who attended her weekly receptions; so the ceremonies had an air of dignity, and yet all hint of pomp was avoided. Martha realized that the attention of the nation was on the President's home, and she was determined that it should in no way reflect the regal display of the monarchy from which America had freed itself.

Few could have filled the difficult position as well as did this daughter of Colonial Virginia, who combined aristocratic culture with a firm faith in the principles of democracy. As mistress of the Executive Mansion, she set a happy example for succeeding First Ladies; and yet she called those years in New York and Philadelphia—to which the capital had been moved in 1790—her "lost days," and explained to a friend: "I had little thought when the war was finished that any circumstances could possibly happen which would call the General into public life again. I had

The Washingtons holding one of the first presidential receptions

anticipated, from that moment, we should be suffered to grow old together in solitude and tranquillity. That was the first and dearest wish of my heart. . . . Yet I cannot blame him for . . . obeying the voice of his country. . . . I am still determined to be cheerful and happy in whatever situation I may be."

For eight years Martha Washington carried the burden of her last public duty, always longing for the plantation home on the Potomac. And when, in 1797, the end of Washington's second term put a close to his public life, Martha was young again in her delight: "The General and I feel like children just released from school . . . and we believe that nothing can tempt us to leave the sacred roof tree again."

Just two years were left to Martha and her husband to enjoy Mount Vernon together, but they were happy years. True, there were no more rides together across plantation fields; no more spirited hunt dinners, as the days of the scarlet riding habit and wide hooped ball gowns were long past. But the new days, the last days, brought a quiet contentment that Martha had long sought: "I am again fairly settled down to the pleasant duties of an old-fashioned Virginia housekeeper, steady as a clock, busy as a bee, and cheerful as a cricket."

Abigail Smith Adams

(1744–1818)

THE first First Lady had come from Virginia, with its wide plantation fields and quiet-flowing rivers, its snug little towns, and its beribboned gentlemen and ladies. The second came from New England, with its dark forests and swift, cold streams and rocky hills, its bleak winters, and its rugged pioneers. The second was stanch Abigail Adams.

Abigail never rode to hounds, never danced at Colonial court balls, nor wintered at Morristown or Valley Forge. Had she been called upon to ride or dance or even march into battle, she would have done so—and done it well—for Abigail Adams had the wit and valor of the true pioneer: what she set her hand to do, she could do.

She was born on November 11, 1744, the daughter of the Reverend William Smith, Congregational minister of Weymouth, Massachusetts, and Elizabeth Quincy Smith. Because she was a frail child, Abigail was never sent to school, but learned her letters in an informal sort of way, curling up in a corner of her father's study to puzzle over his theological books, or visiting Grandmother Quincy, who taught her to knit and spin. In her bib, apron and dark mitts she was a grave little figure as she read and pondered on "duty."

As she grew into girlhood, Abigail was able to join her neighbors in play; on sleigh rides over snow-packed, twisting roads none was merrier than the young girl whose childhood had been so lonely, so serious. Quick to tease but able to laugh when others teased her, spirited Abigail became a favorite in Weymouth. Girls of the village went with their brothers on sleighing or coasting parties, then retreated from the cold of New England winter twilight to meet at her house for mugs of hot tea and plates of gingerbread and apple butter.

Saturday was a particularly busy day, when New Englanders prepared the Sunday meal, so that they could be free to spend most of the Sabbath in church. Early in the morning, Abigail and her mother started to get beef and johnnycake ready, stewed pumpkins and supawn porridge. The open fireplace threw a fragrant mixture of faint wood smoke and warm spicy cooking savors back into the kitchen, as Abigail knitted by the fire and watched steaming pots on the crane.

While Abigail was growing up in Weymouth and Mount Wollaston, young John Adams was working on his father's farm at Braintree, a village near Weymouth; just as soon as he was old enough, he entered Harvard College. He was riding circuit, practicing law in his home district, when he met Abigail. Few approved of John's interest in her. John was a lawyer, and Abigail's family and Weymouth very much objected to his being a lawyer. Like almost everyone else, in those early New England days, they believed that lawyers were a poor sort. Law was a new profession in the eighteenth century; people thought that any man who made his living at the expense of other persons' troubles must be cheap, lazy and, very probably, dishonest. Wey-

mouth could not understand why pretty, educated Abigail, the descendant of a long line of churchmen, should waste her time on "that lawyer, John Adams."

Independent Abigail did not feel that she was wasting her time. She loved John, and he loved her, and she meant to marry him. And in spite of all objections, they were married in 1764.

For ten years their life was uneventful. John's one ambition was to distinguish himself in his profession; but when he was elected a delegate from Massachusetts to a meeting of the tax-burdened Colonies, in 1774, a new life began for him and for Abigail. His part in that first Continental Congress marked the beginning of twenty-three years of public life, a public career which was to raise him from a provincial lawyer to an international statesman.

Isolated on her little farm at Braintree, Abigail made that career possible for him. John was left without means of making a living when England, to punish Boston for its defiant Tea Party, closed the courts. He then had only the Braintree farm; but he could not manage the farm and at the same time work in Boston and Philadelphia for the freedom of the Colonies. With all his heart he wanted to serve the cause of the Revolution. He fiercely believed in justice and liberty, but somehow his wife and children must be supported. All this was troubling him when he wrote to Abigail from Boston: "Let me know what it is best for us to do. It is expensive keeping a family here, and there is no prospect of any business in my way in this town this whole summer. I don't receive a shilling a week."

Practical, loyal Abigail solved the problem. While John served America, she would support the family. In the years that followed, cannon roared across her cornfields, savage

Indians lurked in the nearby woods, disease struck at her children and herself, but she never faltered. The woman who, as a lonely child in Weymouth, had schooled herself to know duty, carried on alone, doing her work just as faithfully as John did his. So well did she manage the farm that, when John retired from the presidency in 1811, it was the Braintree land, developed by Abigail, that provided an income for them.

In the "happy, the peaceful, the elegant, the hospitable, the polite city of Philadelphia," as he described it to Abigail, John worked with Patrick Henry, Lee, Washington, and other leaders to unify the Colonies for their common struggle against England.

Up in Braintree, Abigail tended the dairy, fed stock, worked in the garden, watched over the planting of grain. In the spring, when sap first broke loose from the frost, she sometimes went with her little son John Quincy Adams and the few farm hands to tap maple trees and boil sap for syrup and maple sugar.

Abigail was weather-wise. Often in early spring she stood at the door to study sky and winds, learning from them that in a day or two she would have to begin the planting. And after planting there was cultivating and weeding. In August came the haying. Farm hands set up their grindstones in a shady spot of the orchard, and Abigail could hear the sharp grinding of their scythes against the rough wheel. Hurried, hot days of harvest followed, when the hay was cut swiftly down by scythes and sickles that gleamed in the bright sunlight. At the sound of the dinner horn, the harvesters trooped back to Abigail's farmhouse for the dinner she had cooked, then quickly returned to the fields to finish haying before a storm broke.

But Abigail had not finished. From the dock weed and plantain that grew close to the house, she had to make dyes for her clothes and linens. There was still the winter's supply of soap to be made from tallow and grease saved from butchering and cooking; so she carried wood ashes from the fireplace outside to great iron kettles, then boiled lye and grease into soap. With the help of her three young sons and little Abigail, her daughter, she dipped a number of tallow candles and a few bayberry or beeswax candles for very special use.

In winter, as thick snow covered the fields and drifted high around the house, she spent the days at her loom and spinning wheel. Her hands, square and small, made clothes for the family, shoes out of calamanco—for she would have gone barefooted rather than wear stiff shoes of leather—all the bedding and tablecloths; yet she somehow found time to teach her children. They learned their letters and ciphering just as she had learned them at Grandmother Quincy's fireside, the whir of a spinning wheel sounding through the daily lessons.

By the spring of 1775, the Revolution had marched almost to her own door. The day after the battle of Lexington and Concord, a company of minutemen stopped at the farm, and she gave them her pewter spoons to be melted for bullets. As the fighting closed in around Boston and nearby Braintree, John hastily wrote to Abigail: "In case of real danger . . . fly to the woods with our children." She made no move to desert her post and leave the farm to British invaders, but only replied: "I would not have you distressed about me. Danger, they say, makes people valiant."

Anxiously, she awaited news of neighborhood skirmishes between Royal Marines and minutemen. Her concern was more for the success of the patriot forces than for her own safety. After she had watched a poorly equipped American company march past the farm, she wrote to John: "Courage I know we have in abundance . . . but, powder, where shall we get a sufficient supply?"

He, too, was wondering what could be done to arm and strengthen the Colonial forces. He realized that the Colonies must unite their minutemen companies and place themselves under a single leader. Looking about him at the Philadelphia conference, John decided that Colonel George Washington would make the best leader. Against strong opposition, he worked to make him commander-in-chief. Massachusetts thought that one of its delegates should have the post. New York disagreed, declaring that it should have the honor; and so with all the rest of the Colonies.

Again and again, John impatiently got up from his chair to assert that the delegates were losing precious time in their selfish wrangling. They must, he insisted, choose the man who was best fitted for leadership, no matter from what Colony he came. The fate of all the Colonies depended upon the character of the man they elected commander-in-chief. He ended his argument each time with a demand that Washington be elected. He finally won his case, and could write to Abigail: "I can now inform you that the Congress have made the choice of the modest and virtuous, the amiable, generous, and brave George Washington, Esquire, to be General of the American army. . . ."

Even while he was writing to Abigail of Washington's appointment, a small force of patriots under the command of Colonel Prescott was digging entrenchments on the high land behind Boston. The following day brought the battle of Bunker Hill. Thunder of batteries and muskets summoned Abigail out of the farmhouse. With her son John Quincy she climbed neighboring Penn's Hill to view the battle. Tense, she watched all through the day, seeing the flames of burning Charlestown whip round the entrenchments, swirls of smoke sometimes hiding both patriots and redcoats, but always she could hear the sharp pounding of Royal Navy guns from the bay and the crack of infantry muskets on the hill.

A year later she again went to the top of the hill; but then it was to see Washington's troops victoriously storm Boston from Dorchester Heights, putting the city back into the hands of the Americans. Not long after Boston had been delivered from the British, its citizens met to celebrate momentous news—the Colonies had declared themselves an independent country.

Abigail rode into Boston to hear the Declaration of Independence, and she wrote John: "Last Thursday . . . I went with the multitude into King Street to hear the Proclamation for Independence. . . . The troops appeared under arms, and all the inhabitants assembled there (the small pox prevented many thousands from the country), when Colonel Crafts read from the balcony of the State House the proclamation. . . . As soon as he ended, the cry from the balcony was, 'God save our American States,' and then three cheers rent the air. The bells rang, the privateers fired, the forts and batteries, the cannon were discharged . . . and every face appeared joyful . . . the King's arms were taken down from the State House, and every vestige of him from every place in which it appeared, and burnt in King Street. Thus ends royal authority in this State."

In her letters to John, Abigail made a rugged effort to hide her loneliness; but every so often—after she had dutifully told him that the corn looked good but sugar was four dollars a pound and calico forty dollars a yard—there would be wistfulness in her writing: "I have received a good deal of paper from you. I wish it had been more covered; the writing is very scant, yet I must not grumble. I know your time is not yours or mine. . . . All the letters I receive from you seem to be written in so much haste that they scarcely leave room for a social feeling. They let me know you exist, but some of them contain scarcely six lines. I want some sentimental effusions of the heart."

At last, after long service as director of the Board of War, John was given a short leave of absence. Scarcely had he got back to Braintree and Abigail, when Congress sent him to France to help Benjamin Franklin in getting money and supplies there for the struggling American army. Once more Abigail was left to carry on alone. She did not see John again for three years.

In 1784 he saw no hope of being recalled to America for some time; so he wrote her to join him abroad. She boarded the canvas-rigged *Active*, and on almost the first day out Abigail Adams, who was "a mortal enemy to anything but a cheerful countenance and a merry heart," became seasick, miserably seasick. Her tight little cabin was redolent of oil fumes and the smoke of fermenting potash. The *Active* pitched and tossed and recovered only to roll from rail to rail. "All adds to the *flavor*," commented Abigail as soon as she was well enough to go on deck. There, wrapped in a double calico gown topped by a baize gown and a cloth cloak, she busied herself learning to distinguish a to'gallan's'il from a royal sail, a balloon jib from a flying jib.

"The Captain compliments me," she wrote, "by telling me that he is sure I know well enough how to steer, to take a turn at the helm. I may do pretty well in fair weather, but 'tis your masculine spirits that are made for storms. I love the tranquil scenes of life." Yet, just a few days later when the ship lay becalmed, she contradicted that statement, and unconsciously revealed her lifelong characteristic when she wrote: "I begin to think that a calm is not desirable in any situation in life. Man was made for action and for bustle, too, I believe."

During Abigail's life abroad she had opportunity enough for activity. After several months in France, which she very much disliked, because its extravagance and disregard of dirt irked her New England love of tidiness, she went with John to London. At the Court of St. James's they tried to develop a friendly feeling between the mother country and the new United States of America. Officially, as the first American minister to England, it was John's duty to promote favorable trade and diplomatic relations; but it was Abigail who really smoothed much of the way. She had had no social experience; but she met the strict demands of British court etiquette with a genuine simplicity and tact.

Both John and King George III were brusque. Neither made a notable attempt to placate the other on affairs of state. King George was disappointed in his loss of America; nor did he make an effort to conceal his disappointment. John, almost too outspoken to be a diplomat, was stung by the King's hostile manner. Often he would have shown his anger had not Abigail quietly placed herself as a buffer between the two irritable statesmen.

She resented the royal manner just as much as he did, but she curbed her irritation because she realized that she and John could not allow their personal feelings to hamper the service they were doing America as its official representatives in England. Much as she wanted to rebel, she fastened herself into the prescribed court dress; set a plumed cap on her carefully dressed hair; pinned a bouquet of roses at her waist; and spent trying hours merely being pleasant to everyone. Curtsying, she smiled away her fatigue and her distaste for pomp. Abigail had been a farmer, a house-keeper, a nurse, and now she was a diplomat: what she set her hand to do, she could do.

For three years she punctually attended court balls and presentations. Not once did New England Abigail fawn upon royalty; her amiable courtesy gained her the reluctant admiration of official England. When John and she sailed for America in 1788, they had established in England a respect for their young country. They had made the way easier for succeeding ambassadors.

Back home, John found himself elected Vice-President of the United States, and he served in that office until elected to the presidency in 1797. When the national capital was removed from Philadelphia to Washington, Abigail could not at once join him there, for she had not recovered from a long illness. As soon as she could stand the journey, she got into her chaise and set off for the new city of Washington, a town in the wilderness. Abigail had lived in the capital of England and in the capital of France, and she was the first First Lady to live in Washington, the permanent capital of the United States.

What she saw on her arrival was nothing to remind her of London or of Paris, but rather was a symbol of the youth and enterprise of her own America: "Here and there [she wrote] is a small cot, without a glass window, interspersed among the forests, through which you travel miles without seeing any human being. In the city there are buildings

enough, if they were compact and finished, to accommodate Congress . . . but as they are, and scattered as they
are, I see no great comfort for them. . . . The house [the
Executive Mansion] is upon a grand and superb scale, re-
quiring about thirty servants . . . to keep the apartments
in proper order, and perform the ordinary business of the
house and stables. . . . Surrounded with forests, can you
believe that wood is not to be had, because people cannot
be found to cut and cart it? . . . We have, indeed, come
into a new country. . . . The house is made habitable, but
there is not a single apartment finished. . . ."

The streets were ankle-deep in mud; many of the buildings were still just plans on paper. Pennsylvania Avenue was
a swamp, through which a lane had been chopped from
the tangled alder bushes; a board bridged a gully between
the road and the Executive Mansion; closing in the city
were the thick forests. New and raw was the capital city; but
it was America's own capital; and America, after the gallant, long struggle to make itself a nation, was proud of it.

Confident that the city would some day have all the
beauty America planned for it, Abigail wrote: "It is a beautiful spot, capable of every improvement, and the more I
view it, the more I am delighted with it."

Visitors from neighboring Georgetown and from the
sparsely settled countryside drove into Washington to call
on the First Lady and to see the Executive Mansion, the
"President's Palace." From the friendly ease with which
Abigail greeted them and invited them to her tea table,
none could guess that the President's wife was puzzling on
how to get enough wood to heat the house, or wondering
if the family wash were drying properly in the nearby East
Room.

Poised and unworried though she seemed, she was very glad to leave public life in 1801 and go back to Braintree. Abigail was tired, she was not well, she was no longer young. Since her wedding day in 1764 she had lived according to her belief that "no man prospers without the consent and co-operation of his wife." When John, who had risen to the presidency through her co–operation, no longer needed her active help, she thought she would be glad to rest. She was prepared to enjoy "the tranquil scenes of life"; but New England Abigail was home only a very little while when tranquillity became irksome.

Semi-invalid though she was for the last few years of her life, Abigail watched over her farm and household, knitted, and wrote hundreds of letters famed for ready wit and pungent description. Closest to her heart, however, was the career which her son John Quincy Adams was making for himself. It was Abigail's ambitious hope that "Mr. J.Q.A.," as she called him when she teased, would be able to serve his country as well as had John Adams. Eagerly, she watched the son whom she had taught at her own hearth, who had seen with her the beginning of American freedom on Bunker Hill, steadily advance in national service. She studied his work as Minister to Germany, Russia, and England, and as Senator; and none was happier than she when President Monroe, in 1817, appointed him Secretary of State.

Three years before her son became President of the United States, Abigail died; she would have gloried in seeing "Mr. J.Q.A." in the high office once held by his father, for she knew that John Quincy Adams would serve his country to the best of his ability, just as his father and mother had done.

Martha Jefferson Randolph
(1772–1836)

Maria Jefferson Eppes
(1778–1804)

"Coniunctis exercitibus Latinum," Martha desperately repeated, and hunched closer to Livy's history of the Roman Empire on that bright spring day of 1787 in Paris. Through an open window she could hear light-hearted classmates chattering in lively French as they rollicked through the recreation hour. She wanted to be out there, too, with her own particular chums in the convent, Julia Annesley and Brunette de Chateaubrun. From her desk she could see high, white clouds, could hear the jaunty spring songs of birds, and could feel a lazily drifting wind.

It was all very tempting, and Livy was very dull; yet, even at fifteen, Martha wanted more than anything else to please her father. They had been comrades from the time she had first been able to follow him about at their Virginia plantation home, Monticello. Those days seemed long ago to her, as she sat in the convent schoolroom. The gay spring afternoon reminded her too much of walks and rides she had taken with her father in faraway Virginia; but, in thinking of him, she also remembered that she had promised him only a day or two ago that she would master her Latin. She closed her eyes tightly for a moment to shut out the picture of Monticello and of schoolmates at play in the convent garden, and again began to plod through "Coniunctis exercitibus Latinum primum agrum perpopulati sunt. . . ."

Thomas Jefferson and his daughter had been particularly close to each other from the time Martha was ten, for Mrs. Jefferson had died that year. During the first few weeks after her death he had kept Martha with him every moment, and would see no one else. When he went to Paris as United States Minister to France, he took her abroad with him, putting her to school in the convent of the Abbaye Royale de Panthémont.

At first it was hard for them both in Paris. Martha, who spoke no French, was homesick, and Jefferson was almost broken by the death of his wife. She had been one of the famous belles of Virginia, when he courted her in 1771. Her first husband, Bathurst Skelton, had died a few years earlier, and she had again entered society when Jefferson, violin in hand, used to go over to her home, The Forest, to play minuets with her. There were other suitors there, too, but Jefferson won her, and they were married on New Year's day, 1772.

They drove up the James River, along the Ragged Mountains, to the Rivanna River, then rode on horseback up to Monticello, the "Little Mountain" home that Jefferson had designed and helped to build. Their first child, Martha, was born there on September 27, 1772, and her sister Maria in 1778. Mrs. Jefferson was not strong; at her request, Jefferson refused to leave her to serve in public office, but spent almost all of his time at Monticello. There in his study he read the classic Latin and Greek writers, studied astronomy, natural science, and history, while Martha played near him. When they went for walks, he carried a pocket full of Indian corn for Martha to feed the tame deer that he kept on the plantation.

Except for the time that Jefferson served as Governor of Virginia and in Congress, the family seldom left Monticello. Martha spent her childhood there in the large white house which was filled with novelties of her father's invention. There was the seven-day clock with its weights of cannon balls and its bell of copper and silver; doors that opened mechanically; narrow, twisting stairways tucked out of sight in light shafts; beds that fitted into alcoves or that were drawn up to the ceiling when not in use; a swivel chair on which Martha could twirl giddily whenever her father was not in his study. All the bricks for the house had been made on the plantation; the wood cut and trimmed there; all the nails made in a little factory that Jefferson had set up in one of the farm sheds.

Mrs. Jefferson's death in 1782 halted his work there. Without her, it was hard for him to enjoy Monticello; so he welcomed his appointment as Minister Plenipotentiary to France. Martha and he sailed for Paris in 1784, leaving the six-year-old Maria with her aunt, Mrs. Eppes. Jefferson's first thought, after the arrival in Paris, was to find a suitable school for Martha. He selected the Panthémont, a convent for the daughters of the French nobility and those of the leading foreign diplomats. Madame La Fayette sponsored Martha for admission to the Panthémont, and the little American donned the crimson uniform of the pensioners.

For the first month or two Jefferson visited her daily. He found a very lonely, rather forlorn little girl whose one

thought as she got up each morning in the cheerless dormi-
tory was that her father would be coming to see her that
afternoon. As she gradually learned French and could talk
with her schoolmates, none of whom spoke English, she
grew less homesick and became a favorite at the convent.

Her father, busy as he was at the court of Louis XVI and
Marie Antoinette, kept a close watch over Martha's education. He was particularly anxious to have her work at her
music, and outlined a typical day for her, saying: "from 8
to 10, practise music; from 10 to 1, dance one day and draw
another; from 1 to 2, draw on the day you dance, and write
a letter the next day; from 3 to 4, read French; from 4 to 5,
exercise yourself in music; from 5 until bedtime, read English, write, etc.

"Take care that you never spell a word wrong. Always
before you write, consider how it is spelt, and, if you do not
remember it, turn to a dictionary. It produces great praise
to a lady to spell well."

Nothing in her life was too trivial to interest him. He
wanted to know everything she did at school, everything
she read, what she thought. He even wrote her on the subject of her clothes, reminding her that she was occasionally
lax about her dress: ". . . your wear should be fine of its
kind. But above all things and at all times let your clothes
be neat, whole, and properly put on. Do not fancy you must
wear them until the dirt is visible to the eye; but be you,
from the moment you rise till you go to bed, as cleanly and
properly dressed as at the hours of dinner and tea. I hope,
therefore, the moment you rise from bed, your first work
will be to dress yourself in such style, as that you may be
seen by any gentleman without his being able to discover a
pin amiss or any other circumstance of neatness wanting."

Even while he wrote to Martha, he was thinking, too, of Maria in America with her aunt. Both Martha and he wanted Maria, or Polly, as they called her, to join them in Paris; but she did not want to cross the ocean. Whenever Jefferson pleaded with her to leave Mrs. Eppes and sail for France, he would be answered by one of Polly's determined little notes of placid refusal: "Dear Papa, I should be very happy to see you, but I can not go to France, and hope that you and sister Patsy [her name for Martha] are well. Your affectionate daughter"; or "Dear Papa, I want to see you and sister Patsy, but you must come to Uncle Eppes' house."

Promises of toys and holidays could not move Polly from her refusal to leave America. In desperation, Jefferson decided to employ a ruse to get her to France, and Mrs. Eppes followed the plan that he wrote to her. She coaxed Polly and some of her friends to play aboard one of the ships in the harbor. After an afternoon of hide-and-seek and tag, Polly fell asleep on the deck. The captain put her playmates ashore, quickly ordered the lines cast from the ship, and nosed the boat out to sea. Polly, at her father's orders, had been shanghaied.

Jefferson charged Martha to take care of Polly at the Panthémont, writing her that she must act as a mother to the younger girl, saying: "Teach her always to be true . . . teach her never to be angry."

Not long before Jefferson left his diplomatic post, in 1789, he took Martha, then sixteen, and Polly, ten, out of school. For the first time Martha entered the social world of Paris, the fashionable and witty world in which her father was already a favorite. She made her bow at court before Louis and Marie Antoinette, met the debonair friends of the popular Marquis de La Fayette, and vainly tried to coax her father to let her attend more than three balls a week. There were so many lovely balls to go to, she pleaded, and she loved to dance, particularly to the rollicking music which always distinguished the cotillions at the Duke of Dorset's and Lady Caroline Tufton's.

"Three dances only," Jefferson repeated. "All morning you are at the stay maker's, the hairdresser's, or the milliner's, and in the afternoon you are calling or at garden parties. You must rest some time, you know." He was quite firm in his refusal, but he enjoyed his tall young daughter's eager interest in the new life, and often stood in the door of a ballroom to watch her dance.

In the autumn of 1789 the Jeffersons said farewell to "le bon Paris." After a voyage of thirty days they reached Norfolk and drove down the coast to Monticello. The quiet of the plantation seemed strange after the gala life of Paris, but Martha soon forgot that charming city in a new excitement, the excitement of preparing for her marriage to Thomas Mann Randolph, her second cousin. They had been playmates as children, although they had seen little of each other for the past five years, they had planned to be married as soon as young Randolph finished his education abroad in Edinburgh. He was waiting for Martha when she returned from France, and they were married in February of 1790. The eighteen-year-old bride and her husband stayed at Monticello for a few months, then moved to their own estate, Varina, near Richmond.

Jefferson, then Secretary of State in Washington's cabinet, set himself to direct the education of the twelve-year-old Polly, just as he had directed Martha's. His letters to Polly, who was again staying with Mrs. Eppes, outlined a rigorous schedule of study, but she did her best to follow it, even to seeing the sun rise every day. Her father would ask: "Tell me . . . how many pages you read every day in Don Quixote? . . . whether you repeat a grammar lesson every day; what else you read; how many hours a day you sew; whether you have had an opportunity of continuing your music? whether you know how to make a pudding yet, to cut out a beefsteak, to sow spinach or set a hen?"

Three weeks later the post coach would bring Polly's answer from Virginia to Jefferson in New York: "I read in Don Quixote every day to my aunt, and say my grammar in Spanish and English, and write, and read in Robertson's America. After I am done with that I work till dinner, and a little more after that. My cousin Bolling and I made a pudding the other day. My aunt has given us a hen . . ."

For her reading, Jefferson sent Polly a copy of Anacharsis and Gibbon's *The Decline and Fall of the Roman Empire*, and she dutifully set herself to read them. Jefferson was not always playing the teacher; often enough his colleagues at the capital would see his tall gaunt figure striding into a dress shop to order clothes and materials for Polly or Martha. He even kept them informed about the fashions: "Instead of sending the two veils to your sister and yourself round with the other things, I enclose them with this letter. Observe that one of the strings is to be drawn tight round the root of the crown of the hat, and the veil then falling over the brim of the hat, is drawn by the lower string as tight or as loose as you please round the neck. When the veil is not chosen to be down, the lower string is also tied round the root of the crown, so as to give the appearance of a puffed bandage for the hat. I send also enclosed the green lining for the calash."

Jefferson's daughter Martha served as White House hostess.

In the autumn of 1797 Jefferson, as the shopper for the family, brought a coach full of dresses, hats, gloves, and shoes down to Virginia, for Polly was married that fall to John Wayles Eppes, her cousin and childhood playmate. For five years the young couple spent each summer with Jefferson at Monticello, where the Randolphs joined them for the holiday. Those few weeks together each year were not enough for Jefferson; he wanted his daughters and their families to be with him at the Executive Mansion.

Finally, in October of 1802, Martha wrote that Polly and she would visit him, but before they set off in their coach would he please "be so good as to send orders to the milliner . . . for two wigs of the color of the hair enclosed, and of the most fashionable shapes, that they may be in Washington when we arrive."

Martha was in society for the first time since she had left the glittering court of Louis XVI. She had spent twelve years on her Virginia plantation; and, busy as she had been, she sometimes hungered for the music and brilliance of Parisian society. Her Washington visit lasted only two months; but, with Dolley Madison as guide, she crowded a round of balls, teas, afternoon calls, and dinners into her brief stay.

That visit was the last that Polly made to her father at the capital. She died two years later. Once again, Jefferson turned to Martha for comfort, just as he had done when Mrs. Jefferson died. The widowed Martha took her family, six daughters and one son, to live with Jefferson at the Executive Mansion in Washington.

When Jefferson retired from the presidency, she accompanied him to Monticello. They were home again, home in the white pillared house in the Ragged Mountains. Behind them was the Blue Ridge range. In front, the tidewater lowlands. Home again, Martha and her father; but they were changed, and Monticello was changed. From time to time the house had been enlarged until, at Jefferson's retirement from public life, it had thirty-five rooms. It was still "home," but so constantly filled by visitors that it seemed almost an inn. From the moment Jefferson and Martha's family returned from Washington, men and women from all parts of the country and even from Europe journeyed to Monticello to see the former president. The Duke de la Rochefoucauld, the Marquis de Chastellux, La Fayette, and former colleagues all drove up through the sticky red clay to Monticello where they dined, stayed the night, and often remained for several days or weeks. At one time Martha had to prepare accommodations for fifty guests. For seventeen years, until Jefferson's death, they extended boundless hospitality.

Their generosity lost Monticello for them. Throughout his public life, Jefferson had neglected his private affairs for those of the nation; his fortune consequently suffered. The cost of entertaining all who came to see him consumed the remainder. At his death, Martha had to leave Monticello. She took refuge at the Boston home of her daughter, Mrs. Coolidge; but she could not forget Monticello, and she wrote: "The approach of spring makes my heart turn to dear home . . . only to remember that I have no home." And, "Oh, how often the words 'dear home' tremble upon my lips and dim my eyes! Will it ever again be my home?"

Except for a brief stay in 1828, it was no longer Martha's home, for Monticello was sold in December. Her father and her home were gone; eight years later Martha died, and was buried on the mountainside at Monticello.

Dorothea (Payne) Todd Madison
(1772–1849)

HUNDREDS of tall candles lighted the Executive Mansion, and quick laughter broke through the sparkling Mozart melody to which the dancers were circling in a minuet.

Outside, along Pennsylvania Avenue, a line of carriages faltered through mud and sink holes, carrying scores who were still on their way to the President's house. Jolted by every lurch of the wheels, the ladies clung to the carriage side straps with one hand and steadied their plumed turbans with the other. Flecks of mud spotted their cloaks and spattered against the knee breeches and silk hose of their escorts. Neither the hectic ride nor the mud could make them turn back, for they were on their way to Dolley Madison's levee, where all Washington met. When "Queen Dolley" entertained, political jealousies were laid aside in the charm of her hospitality, and Washington forgot that it was "a city in the wilderness."

Unlike her predecessors, Martha Washington and Abigail Adams, Dolley Madison thoroughly enjoyed her position as First Lady. Throughout the eight years of her regime, all Washington enjoyed it with her. As she made her way among the dancers, glowing and stylish in em-

broidered satin, plumed turban, and pearls, it seemed as though the world of gay fashion must always have been her world. But until she was twenty-two, Dolley had moved in quite another world, that quiet and secluded one which the Quakers built for themselves.

For the young Dolley there had been no parties, no satin gowns. Scotchtown, the Payne plantation where she spent her childhood, was in a lonely part of the Virginia tidewater country. As Quakers, the Paynes did not take part in the occasional hunt dinners and balls. Their home was large and richly furnished, and they were generous with hospitality for the few visitors who made the long journey to the plantation; yet they lived simply and very much within themselves. Dolley's brother and sisters were her only companions, and they turned to her for leadership. They followed her gladly, not just because she was older. If they admired something she had, she shared it with them, gave it to them when they would take it. If one fell in a game, it was Dolley who first stopped to help. Not often were there quarrels, but when there were, Dolley was the one who made peace with a challenge to race down to the field where the new colt was learning to walk on slender, trembling legs.

As she led them in games of her own invention, she looked demure enough in apron, kerchief, finger mitts, and laced slippers. A hood covered her black wayward curls, and a linen complexion mask almost hid her laughing eyes; but, nestled beneath her kerchief was a tiny pouch of jewelry, a secret present from her grandmother. When she was not playing, Dolley lifted the jewels from their hiding place to admire them as she dreamed of a day when she might, perhaps, wear them. Meanwhile there were lessons to be learned and games to be played at lonely Scotchtown.

One day, when she was eleven, Dolley and her little band made final visits to the gray hickory trees, down near the pasture, where they scooped a few last nuts into their pockets; to the field where they had so often hunted fat strawberries. No one seemed to notice their absence from the mansion house. Father and Mother were busy directing the loading of trunks and furniture onto the waiting wagons, but at last a slave blew the field horn to summon the children, and they were bundled into a coach for the long journey to Philadelphia, their new home.

For the first few years in the North they lived very much as they had at Scotchtown, attended by servants who had refused their liberty when Mr. Payne freed his plantation slaves. Each year, however, he lost more of his fortune; so Dolley spent more of her time at home to help care for the household. One of those who tried to save Mr. Payne's business was John Todd, a young Quaker lawyer. When Mr. Payne realized that his business failure would leave his family practically penniless, he encouraged Dolley to favor John's suit for her hand, although she had been heard to say she meant never to marry. To relieve her father of worry, she accepted the earnest young Friend.

John came for his eighteen-year-old bride, who was prettier than some of the Quakers thought seemly, and was married to her in 1790. Throughout the three quiet years of that marriage she did not regret her decision to become Mistress Todd. John and she lived very simply; but Dolley was happy in her home on South Fourth Street, content in the company of her husband and son, John Payne Todd. The ability to fit herself into any situation gave Dolley almost lifelong happiness. She lived in the moment. She never glanced at the past, never questioned the future. If once, as a little girl, she had held some old-fashioned jewelry tightly in her hand and pictured the day when she would wear it, she no longer thought of it. She had her home, John, and her little son, and she was happy.

Yellow fever scourged Philadelphia in the summer of 1793. Among its victims was John Todd, who succumbed to the fever after tireless weeks of aiding stricken relatives and friends.

At his death, Dolley went to live at her mother's house. Both her husband and her father were dead, but she did not have a great deal of time to brood. Mrs. Payne was supporting the family by boarding several members of Congress, and Dolley shared the work with her. Aaron Burr, brilliant, ambitious, and cynical, was one of the lodgers, and it was he who introduced Dolley to James Madison. The "Widow Todd" at once recognized the merit of "the great little Madison." She knew his reputation for shyness; she knew he was thought to be coldly reserved; but as he visited with her in the parlor of the boarding house, she led him to talk of himself and was won by his courteous charm. Nor could he keep hidden his gentle humor when Dolley, winsome in mulberry satin and crisp white kerchief, teased him about his reputation for gravity.

Most of Philadelphia interested itself in the courtship because of Madison's prominence; even the President and Mrs. Washington smiled approval when Madison and Dolley were married in September of 1794.

Dolley's second marriage, performed in a Church of England ceremony, was very different from the simple Quaker reading that had made her the wife of John Todd. Then, John and she, in Quaker dress, had merely stood up together in meeting and spoken the brief words that made them man and wife. At her marriage to James Madison, Dolley withdrew from the subdued Quaker group in which she had lived. After a month at Montpellier, Madison's estate in the Blue Ridge country, they returned to Philadelphia where, at the height of Mrs. Washington's regime as First Lady, Dolley entered the fashionable world she was soon to lead.

All of the smart frivolity of the Philadelphia to which this marriage introduced her was new to Dolley. Formerly, in that same city she had left her home only to market or visit her mother, to attend meeting or join her husband John on summer outings at Gray's Ferry on the Schuylkill. Now, scented and powdered, she drank tea with Mrs. Washington, lunched and dined with the socially prominent; and all the time she was quietly observing how society carried itself. In assembly balls and in the levees at the President's mansion, she found a new world and made it her own.

Because of political differences with John Adams, the incoming President, the Madisons left Philadelphia for Montpellier, where they remained until Thomas Jefferson took office in 1801. Dolley made her second social entrance when President Jefferson appointed Madison his Secretary of State. Jefferson had no official hostess for the Executive Mansion in Washington; but the Madisons and he were intimate friends, and it was not long before he relied upon Dolley to act as First Lady.

All of the state dinners and receptions were held at the Executive Mansion, with the President and Dolley presiding in model "Jeffersonian simplicity," yet the real social center of Washington from 1801 to 1809 was not in the

Mansion but in Dolley's own drawing room. Senators, cabinet members and foreign diplomats met there every day. Out of these popular salons at "Dolley Madison's house" grew strong political alliances for James Madison. Those alliances helped him to victory in the elections of 1808. When he was inaugurated in March of 1809 as fourth President of the United States, Dolley became First Lady of the Land, an honor which had been hers unofficially through Jefferson's administrations.

As soon as she was established in the Executive Mansion, she cheered it with new furnishings—yellow satin for the audience room, a pianoforte, a gold and crystal centerpiece for the state dining table—and enlivened it with her celebrated hospitality. Everyone was welcomed into "Queen Dolley's house" where statesmen found themselves, at a guiding word from her, cordially discussing the sights of Washington with delighted visitors from farms. Dolley was as generous and simple mannered as she had been at Scotchtown. Ability to make each of her guests feel at home was the charm of her hospitality. She never forgot a name or a face, and for everyone she met she had special words of friendliness. No one could irritate her into a quarrel: if there were a disturbance, she simply left the room for a few moments, then returned and resumed conversation as though there had been no threat of unpleasantness. Once she explained, "I would rather fight with my hands than with my tongue."

Friends turned with a smile when they felt the familiar tap of her snuffbox on their shoulders as she passed; they gathered eagerly round her to join the fun. Strangers at the levees looked shyly about to catch sight of the beloved Dolley. Embarrassment vanished when "Her Majesty," as some still called the First Lady in an old-fashioned way, led them to a refreshment table, asked how they fared on the journey to Washington, and told of her own experiences in the new capital. She talked animatedly, but she listened earnestly to all that was said to her: the unfortunate had her sympathy and her aid; the brilliant, her admiration; the witty, her pleasant laugh. All were her friends.

Her popularity helped win re-election for James Madison, who was voted to a second presidential term in spite of the nation's disapproval of the naval war with England. Unlike Abigail Adams, Dolley had little interest in politics, but she was intensely interested in her husband. So long as he wanted a political career she set herself to help him make a success of it. She ignored all controversy on political questions and devoted herself to making friends.

No greater aid could she have given James Madison. He had wealth, political training, and a finely developed mind. What he lacked was the ability, which both Washington and Jefferson had shown, to draw a large following of friends and political supporters. Jefferson and General Washington had a genial, open-hearted manner that attracted the admiration of the nation. "Pale, reflective Madison" was retiring, of delicate health, reserved. He made no effort to meet people even halfway. To Dolley, on the contrary, no effort was too great to make everyone feel at ease and contented. Even if she had not been the wife of an ambitious statesman, she would have been surrounded by friends who were won by her thoughtfulness and generosity, for Dolley Madison found her fulfillment in making others happy.

With Queen Dolley as its hostess, the Executive Mansion—its dining table piled high with pheasants, Virginia hams, and fruit, its rooms alive with music and laughter and candlelight—drew all Washington to its doors until one day, August 23, 1814, when everyone but the First Lady and her servants deserted it. News had reached the city that the British were marching upon Washington, bringing the war into the capital itself. The residents flung their belongings into wagons, pushcarts, and rigs of all sorts, and, panic-stricken, fled the town. President Madison had left earlier to inspect the American forces at Bladensburg, where a handful of troops tried to stem the British invasion.

Dolley stayed at the Mansion, almost alone in the defenseless house. While waiting for news from the battle-field, she busied herself collecting her husband's state papers and in writing to her sister:

Tuesday, August 23, 1814.

Dear Sister,—My husband left me yesterday morning to join General Winder. He inquired anxiously whether I had courage and firmness to remain in the Presidential house till his return, and on my assurance that I had no fear but for him and the success of our army, he left me, beseeching me to take care of myself and of the cabinet papers, public and private. I have since received two dispatches from him. . . . The last is alarming, because he desires I should be ready at a moment's warning to enter my carriage and leave the city; that the enemy seemed stronger than had been reported, and that it might happen that they would reach the city with intention to destroy it. . . . I am accordingly ready. I have pressed as many cabinet papers into trunks as to fill one carriage. Our private property must be sacrificed, as it is impossible to procure wagons for its transportation. . . . My friends are all gone; even Colonel C., with his hundred men, who were stationed as a guard in this inclosure.

Wednesday

Three o'clock

. . . we have had a battle or skirmish near Bladensburg, and I am still here within sound of the cannon. . . . Our kind friend, Mr. Carroll, has come to hasten my departure, and is in a very bad humor with me, because I insist on waiting until the large picture of General Washington is secured, and it requires to be unscrewed from the wall. This process was found to be too tedious for these perilous moments; I have ordered the frame to be broken and the canvas taken out. . . . And now, dear sister, I must leave this house, or the retreating army will make me a prisoner in it, by filling up the road I am directed to take. When I shall again write to you, or where I shall be tomorrow, I cannot tell.

For two unhappy days Dolley and James Madison, First Lady and President of the United States, hunted refuge in the countryside around Washington; then, at the retreat of the invaders, rode back to the capital, a city scarred by flames. The British raiders had burned the Capitol, the Treasury building, and the Executive Mansion. Their home destroyed, the Madisons took over Octagon House. There the exuberant city met to celebrate the news of peace in December of 1814; from there Dolley waved to the returning American soldiers who cheered her as they marched past, home from "Madison's war."

At the end of President Madison's second term, Dolley left the capital, not to return until 1837, twenty years later. Back at Montpellier she tucked away the satin and ermine of her Washington days, the jewels and plumes, and devoted herself to the care of her husband and his mother. Except for a few visits to Monticello, where Jefferson always kept ready the "Madison chamber," Dolley was seldom out of Mother Madison's call. "I am feeble and helpless and owe everything to *her*," Mrs. Madison once said, pointing to Dolley. "She is *my* mother now."

Guests from all parts of the country and Europe visited Montpellier, where they were as welcome as they had been at the Executive Mansion. So generous was Montpellier hospitality that, like Monticello, the estate suffered from the vast cost of housing hundreds of guests. Much of Madison's fortune was dissipated before his death in 1836.

Dolley had stubbornly fought against ill health so that she might nurse her husband. At his death, she suffered a collapse, and her physician ordered her to another climate. At sixty-five, Dolley Madison returned to Washington—not to the Executive Mansion, but to a little house on Lafayette Square. Congress voted her the franking privilege and, as a special honor, the privilege of a seat on the floor of the House of Representatives, the first such favor ever accorded a woman. Congress did more than grant honors to her; it saved her from poverty. Her wastrel son John Payne Todd, to whom Madison and she had given every advantage of education and travel, spent what remained of her fortune, even proceeds from a forced sale of Montpellier; so Congress provided her with money by purchasing James Madison's papers and letters.

In charm and gaiety she was still Queen Dolley. White-haired, she still reigned over the capital, giving help to others when she could—and, with brave serenity, receiving help. Pride kept her, who in days of fortune had been lavish with gifts, from refusal when friends slipped into her pantry with little presents of food and dainties. None dared censure in her hearing the son whose extravagances had forced her into dependency on Congress.

Courage as well as loyalty was in the apology she once

made for him: "My poor boy. Forgive his eccentricities, for his heart is all right." She had been ambitious for him, but she was loyal to him even after he had wasted his talents and opportunities. Few realized that, in all of the gaiety which surrounded her, Dolley found no compensation for the sorrow brought by her son. Only once did she reveal her heartbreak, and that was when she stirred a young niece from a momentary unhappiness by quietly saying: "My dear, do not trouble about it; there is nothing in this world really worth caring for. Yes, believe me, I who have lived so long repeat to you, there is nothing in *this* world really worth caring for."

None could sense heartbreak as Dolley, brave in the lustrous silks and turbans of her White House days, presided in her tiny drawing room much the same as though she were still First Lady. For twelve years she kept her home open to all with the wide welcome she had shown in the Executive Mansion. Statesmen and visitors gathered at her tea table to be received in a gallantry of manner, a warmth of friendliness. On New Year's day and on the Fourth of July, when the President held public receptions, as soon as people had paid their respects to him they hurried to Lafayette Square to greet Dolley Madison. Never was she more proudly hailed than on the night in 1849 when she attended a levee at the White House and passed through the crowded rooms on the arm of President Polk. Six months later, the most glamorous of all First Ladies died in the little house on Lafayette Square.

Elizabeth Kortright Monroe

(1768–1830)

In a flourish of jingling reins, Elizabeth Kortright Monroe, wife of the American Minister to France, drove up to the the door of La Petite Force prison in Paris one day in 1795. While the liveried footman climbed down from the box, she did not stir until the prison guards had noticed the shield of the United States glistening on the carriage door.

Then, her heart hammering, she stepped to the stone street. Her head was erect, her mouth firm, and her poise gave no hint of the fear that she was feeling. Her voice was steady, assured, as she demanded, "Madame La Fayette, if you please. Yes, the marquise who is under sentence of death. I wish to see her at once."

The insolent stare of the Terrorist guard changed into a look of respect and, laying aside his pike, he immediately led her to the marquise.

"Madame Monroe! But you should not have come here. Your visit may get you into great trouble," she cried, catching Elizabeth's hands in her own.

Quietly, Elizabeth reassured her. "This is the only way that Mr. Monroe and I can help, the only way we can show our gratitude for the help your husband gave our country in its time of need." Almost whispering, for the guard was still listening, she continued: "Mr. Monroe can do nothing directly because of his state position; but we believe, my dear marquise, that my visit to you this afternoon will call the attention of the Terrorist government to our interest in you; and Mr. Monroe believes that it will be of benefit to you, unofficial though the visit is."

When the distracted marquise protested that the Monroes were courting censure from their own country by challenging the French government, Elizabeth comforted her, saying there was no danger—although she knew that there was. "But whatever befalls James and me will be worth this risk, if only we can save Madame La Fayette," she told herself as she walked away from the cell and out of the prison. "The unhappy marquise! France has no greater patriot than La Fayette, yet the Terrorists drive him into exile and imprison his wife."

In her carriage again, Elizabeth was driven down the cobblestone street at a smart trot. She had made her departure, too, in a flourish.

A few days later she learned that her visit had been successful. Just as James and she had hoped, the French government had been sufficiently impressed to release the marquise, as a gesture of friendship for America.

Although she had carried off her adventure so dramatically, it was not like Elizabeth to do things with a flourish. Because of her tall, dark beauty she never needed to draw attention to herself. She had been one of the prettiest and most popular girls in New York, and easily took her place at the European courts. She was as much at home in Madrid and at St. James's and St. Cloud, where she was called "La Belle Américaine," as she had been in New York.

Her father, Lawrence Kortright, was one of the founders of the New York Chamber of Commerce. His home was always open to his friends, and Elizabeth grew up in an atmosphere of hospitality. Landowners from up the river would journey into town to stop with the Kortrights. In winter, they came in their coaches, attended by liveried postilions and outriders; in summer, they sailed down the Hudson in their sloops.

When Elizabeth was eighteen she was introduced to a new visitor at the Kortright home. He was young James Monroe, a member of Congress, who had left college in the days of the Revolution to serve with the Continental Army. After the war, he had studied law with Thomas

Jefferson, then served in the Virginia Legislature before entering Congress.

He had crowded a great deal into his twenty-eight years, and his experiences gave him a certain earnest, confident manner that charmed Elizabeth. In the time he could take from his work he followed her to dances; to picnics on the Battery; on sleigh rides up country; and she enjoyed it. They were married in 1786, moving to Fredericksburg, Virginia, then going to France eight years later when James was made Minister Plenipotentiary at Paris.

When they arrived in the turbulent French capital, they found that Robespierre had been executed and that the Reign of Terror was coming to an end although some of its victims, including Madame La Fayette, were still in prison. James was determined to save her even though such an act were beyond his power as American ambassador. He discussed plan after plan with Elizabeth but could hit upon no means of rescue until she volunteered to visit the marquise in prison, and that plan was successful.

Those last days of the Jacobins—the group responsible for the Reign of Terror—were stormy ones in Paris; so Elizabeth at once sent her seven-year-old daughter Eliza to a school where Hortense Eugénie de Beauharnais, stepdaughter of Napoleon, was a pupil. Most of the students were of the French nobility, and the Terrorists had threatened them at first. Napoleon, however, extended his protection to the school as soon as Hortense de Beauharnais was enrolled there; so Elizabeth Monroe was satisfied that Eliza was at the safest school in France.

After two years in Paris, the Monroes were recalled to America, partly because of their action in rescuing Madame La Fayette and partly because James seemed too enthusiastic in his support of the French Revolution. Then there were years of jaunting here and there, again to Paris for the Louisiana Purchase treaty, to the Spanish court at Madrid, to the Court of St. James's in London, back to America and, in 1817, to Washington and the Executive Mansion.

It was not the Executive Mansion that Abigail Adams, Martha Jefferson, and Dolley Madison knew. The British troops had burned all the furnishings in their raid during the War of 1812; flames had blackened the walls. When Congress saw the stained and scarred President's home, it ordered the structure to be painted white, and almost overnight the mansion became the White House.

As Elizabeth and James examined the deserted rooms, they realized new furnishings were needed; so they installed their own furniture, silverware, and china—which the government later bought from them for permanent use in the White House—and ordered a number of additional pieces from France.

When Elizabeth, regal in satin, pearls, and a plumed turban, received at the New Year's reception in 1818, hundreds of guests eagerly examined the renovated White House. They went from room to room, inspecting the richly massed mahogany furniture and bronze ornaments in one part of the mansion, glancing at the delicately carved French pieces in another; chandeliers and sconces gleamed above colored silk curtains. Her guests were very much interested in the White House, and wished that Elizabeth would entertain more than she did. After eight years of Dolley Madison's open-handed hospitality, Washington considered the Executive Mansion its own and the First Lady its own particular hostess.

Even if her health had permitted, Elizabeth probably

would not have carried out the hearty social plan that Dolley had inaugurated. She was much like Martha Washington in her preference for private life. Her first move, as First Lady, was to announce that she would be very glad to receive all visitors, but that she would not, could not, return visits. Residents of the city had remarked that Queen Dolley had ruined her health by dutifully repaying a score of calls a day; but as soon as they heard Elizabeth's announcement they forgot Dolley's ruined health and hotly criticized the "snobbery" of the new First Lady.

Elizabeth was sensitive to the criticism, but she held to her decision, and Washington gradually realized that she was not strong enough to endure a rigorous social life. Slowly, Elizabeth and the city became friends, but the city found it harder to accept her daughter Eliza. Talented and imperious Eliza could not seem to forget that she had once been at school with the nobility of France and had been a companion of Hortense de Beauharnais, Queen of Holland. Washington resented Eliza's vanity, but sensibly dismissed her from its mind to give attention to Elizabeth, whom visitors found cordial and unaffected by her court life.

Her younger daughter Maria was married in 1820 at the first White House wedding ceremony for a President's daughter. At the New Year's reception for the following year, Elizabeth was assisted by both Eliza and Maria. As the crowd moved past Elizabeth, whose shoulders were as white against her velvet gown as the pearls and curved plume in her hair, many murmured, "La Belle Américaine," just as the Parisians had whispered it a quarter of a century earlier. Her beauty was complemented by her daughters—Maria dressed in white satin embroidered with silver thread, and the imperious Eliza in crimson velvet tied with a gold cord.

Her part in the social pageant of Washington tired Elizabeth, however, and James wrote to Jefferson in 1824: "I shall be heartily glad when the term of my service expires, and I may return home in peace with my family, on whom, and especially on Mrs. Monroe, the burdens and cares of my long public service have borne too heavily."

He refused to be considered for a third term but returned with Elizabeth to Oak Hill, their Virginia home, in 1825. For thirty-nine years they had served America together, the tall, earnest Virginian and La Belle Américaine.

Louisa Johnson Adams
(1775–1852)

Louisa nodded and waved her tiny flowered sunshade to answer the greeting of a friend in a passing sedan chair. John Quincy Adams, the slim young man walking beside her, did not notice that anyone had spoken to them. He only knew that he was at Louisa's side again.

For three years, ever since he had first met her in her London home and then left for The Hague to begin work in the American diplomatic service, he had thought a great deal of the tall, dark-haired girl. Not until he had been made Ambassador to Prussia, in 1797, did he judge himself in a position to marry. As soon as he received news of his appointment to the Prussian court of King Frederick Wilhelm III, he hurried back to London and Louisa, and began earnest courtship.

They had much in common, talented Louisa and the studious young son of John and Abigail Adams. Both had lived in England and France; both enjoyed books and plays and music; both had grown up in homes where the family took an intimate part in politics. Louisa's father Joshua Johnson, brother of the first governor of Maryland, had left

America before the Revolution to enter business in London. He married Catherine Nuth, an English girl, and Louisa was born in London in 1775. Later Mr. Johnson was appointed American Consul.

In 1794 John Quincy Adams, recent graduate of Harvard College and quite attractive with his elegant dress and manners, went also to London, stopping for a brief visit before going to The Hague. Louisa was nineteen then, tall and slender-waisted in hooped gown and satin jacket. Once he had met her, John did not forget her. Nor did she forget him. When he returned in 1797, they had only a few days of courtship before they were married on the morning of July 26, 1797, at the parish church of All Hallows.

In October they went to Berlin where John would be the first American Ambassador to Prussia. They were at the city gate when their driver suddenly pulled up the coach. A young Prussian lieutenant thrust his head into the carriage, demanding to know their business. When he was answered that John was "the minister from the United States of America," he was bewildered and asked, "What *are* the United States of America?" John, who had been schooled since childhood in the lore of America, was so surprised by the question that he could not reply for a moment. While he stared in amazement at the lieutenant, a private soldier saluted the puzzled officer and explained that the United States was that new country across the ocean. With a click of the heels and a deep bow from the waist, the Prussian indicated his apology to John and waved the coach on to Berlin.

Frederick Wilhelm III, who succeeded his father on the throne during the Adamses' stay in Germany, was very hospitable. With his queen, Frederick received the young

couple at court, and a pleasantly informal friendship grew
between the royal pair and the Adamses.

They had been four years at Frederick Wilhelm's court
when John's father, who was retiring from the presidency of
the United States, recalled them from Prussia, fearing similar action on the part of Thomas Jefferson, the political
rival who was to succeed him as President.

On return to America the couple made their home in
Boston where John practiced law, but they moved to Washington two years later when he entered the Senate. In the
capital, still a city of mud and swamps, Louisa at once established a salon which rivaled Dolley Madison's in popularity.
Her life in London, in France, and at the Prussian court
was always of interest to the women of Georgetown and
Washington who gathered almost daily for Louisa's teas,
and "conversation parties."

In 1809 John was again appointed to a diplomatic post;
so, with their two-year-old son Charles, Louisa and he once
more set out for a strange country, journeying to the Russian court of St. Petersburg.

Very different from the sun-warmed German land was
chill, dark Russia; and very different from the hearty, com-
panionable Prussian court was the barbaric splendor of im-
perial St. Petersburg. The damp, wind-swept cold closed
round Louisa, and she felt lost in the harsh land. John,
reared in stern New England, was less unhappy, and at once
set himself to learn the language, a tongue which Louisa
never mastered although she was thoroughly at home in
German and French.

They took an apartment on the Nevsky Prospect and
struggled to make John's salary fit their household expenses.
In despair, they found that custom demanded they must

have a steward, a cook, two scullions, a porter, two footmen, a muzhik "to make the fires," a coachman, postilion, valet, personal maid, chambermaid, housemaid, and laundry maid, and must feed and house the families of all. Louisa spent much of her time trying to find ways in which to economize. Often she would be bent over a pad of figures when royal messengers brought invitations to court fêtes. She went to as many as she could afford to buy clothes for and dined off gold plates, wondering meanwhile how she could manage to pay her butcher's bill at the end of the week.

But Emperor Alexander I, Queen Elizabeth, and the Empress Mother received the Adamses as cordially as though Louisa were wearing the tiara of royalty and John the jewels and ribbons of a courtier. Alexander danced the polonaise with Louisa, and always stopped to talk with John on his daily walks in the city. The independence and candor of the Americans charmed the Emperor and his suite.

For Louisa, however, court parties gave little relief in a bleak land where winter began in October and rivers lay white and frozen until April. Hunched at her charcoal burner or reaching high to paste strips of paper over the windows to shut out the sharp cold, she longed for the day when John and she could escape Russia. He was ordered to Ghent, in the autumn of 1813, and Louisa was already wildly packing the trunks when he told her that she was to stay in St. Petersburg, as he expected to get through the treaty-making at Ghent quickly and return to his Russian post.

Alone with her six-year-old son, Louisa forlornly waited in St. Petersburg, watching the Emperor's troops march away to the frontiers to battle the scourging armies of Napoleon. Alexander had already left the city to command his forces in the field, and there were no more fêtes at his court. Russia, a fighting Russia, was grim in its war mood and its snow-driven, sunless days.

For seven months Louisa awaited John's return. When the post finally brought word that she was to join him in Paris, she hired a traveling coach, and with her son set off to cross battle-torn Europe. The northern roads were still packed hard with ice, lined by snowdrifts; so the wheels of the coach were replaced by sled runners. In this way, it went lumbering on toward Paris, while Louisa and Charles ate bites of their frozen provisions, black bread, and hard chunks of cheese.

Just beyond the Russian frontier they left the icy roads; the sled runners were exchanged for wheels. That change meant more to Louisa than a mere speeding of the coach; it meant that she was leaving behind her the hated dark cold of the north country. As she neared Paris she smiled contentedly at the signs of approaching spring—thawing ground, crackled ice thinning in the streams—and thought happily of living again in a land where the sun was more than just a dim, uncertain splotch of light in a heavy sky.

But as she dreamed of Paris and its springtime, a shouted "Halt!" shattered her reverie. Thrown almost from the seat as the driver pulled up the coach horses, she caught Charles tightly against her side, then looked out of the window. All around the coach were soldiers, their face flushed with excitement, their eyes bold and challenging, their hands eagerly gripping swords and guns. In the moment that she watched them silently, realizing they were looking for trouble, they shouted and the cry was, "Vive l'Empéreur! Vive Napoléon!"

"Long live Napoleon, long live the Emperor," repeated

Louisa in a whisper, and her eyes darkened with fright, for she was surrounded by the guard of Napoleon who had recently escaped from Elba and was even then marching upon Paris. "Long live Napoleon!" and on her carriage was the insignia of Russia, the nation that had helped to drive Napoleon into exile on Elba. The French soldiers, mad with joy at Napoleon's return, glared at the Russian coach as though they would tear it to pieces.

As they pressed closer to it, an officer strode through the group and commanded Louisa to tell her business. In perfect French she answered that she was the wife of an American statesman, John Quincy Adams, on her way from St. Petersburg to join him in Paris, beautiful Paris. Her diplomatic tribute to Paris and her correct French won her permission to continue the journey but with a warning to avoid the main roads, which would be filled with troops on the march to join Napoleon. She might, the officer significantly added, have more difficulty in getting through the lines the next time she drove head on into riotous troops.

She traveled the back roads into Paris, arriving in time to witness the feverish hilarity of the Hundred Days, that frenzied interlude between Napoleon's return from Elba and his defeat at Waterloo. Louis XVIII and the royal family had fled; Napoleon had entered Paris the same evening, cheered by soldiers who still wore the fleur-de-lis of the retreating Bourbons on their helmets and belt buckles.

With John, Louisa watched boisterous crowds dancing in the streets; went to the cathedral and saw a throng storming at the doors to catch a glimpse of Napoleon at mass; attended the theater and heard the audience hail him as he entered his box.

By June, Louisa had left turbulent Paris, for John had

been appointed Minister to England. There in London, the city of her girlhood, she saw the climax to the Hundred Days, days that had started so brilliantly for Napoleon and had ended in his crushing defeat at Waterloo by Marshal Blücher and the Duke of Wellington. London celebrated Wellington's triumph with a flaring display of lights in the illuminated words, "Victory," "Wellington and Blücher"; and, as Louisa watched, she thought again of the exultant soldiers who, just a few weeks earlier, had clamored "Vive Napoléon!"

After Waterloo, the Court of St. James's resumed its program of majestic and very solemn dinners and balls. Louisa and John found themselves much in the same uncomfortable position that Abigail and the older John Adams had occupied while serving as American representatives to England, thirty years earlier. Then, England had been hostile because of the Revolution. It was hostile toward the younger Adams because of the recently fought naval War of 1812. But, like Abigail and the older John, Louisa and her husband pitted their wits against the unfriendly Prince Regent, who was acting for his father, George III, and his court.

At the opening of Parliament, Louisa and John joined the crowds on the streets to watch the Prince Regent and his retinue parade to the state buildings. Eight cream-colored horses, decorated with sky-blue ribbons and harnessed in gold leather, pulled the gilded royal coach, while a troop of Horse Guards cleared the way with drawn swords. In one corner of the glittering coach sat the listless Prince Regent, idly glancing at the cheering throng. He seemed just as uninterested when John saw him at the rout which Mrs. Wellesley Pole gave for him and at garden parties at the palace which Louisa scrupulously attended. But then, as John thoughtfully noted in his diary, the music at Mrs. Pole's rout was very melancholy and the company very stiff; and, as for the garden parties, Louisa felt that she could scarcely blame the Prince Regent for his boredom, because she felt much the same way herself. Like diplomatic Abigail, however, she concealed it, even though she earnestly wished she were in her own garden, sketching, or at the harp in her drawing room.

For two years they wisely followed in the footsteps of the older Adamses; then, in 1817, President Monroe appointed John his Secretary of State, and they returned to Washington. Back in her home on F Street, Louisa resumed her salons and Saturday-night cotillions. John took little or no part in the entertaining, preferring to shut himself in his room to read or write, or to walk through the city and along the Potomac. One night, however, he was present, and so was almost everyone else in Washington, for Louisa was giving a triumphal ball for Andrew Jackson, the soldier hero of the hour. For days Louisa had been festooning the house, moving furniture from several rooms in order to accommodate hundreds of guests. Even while she arranged her home, hired musicians and caterers, Washington talked of the party and stormed dressmakers, tailors, hairdressers, jewelers, and frantically ordered the latest powders and scents from Philadelphia. The merry regime of Dolley Madison had returned for a night, and Washington was going to make the most of it.

On the day of the ball the city was enjoying itself in a delightful excitement, and eagerly reading verses that a newspaper, *The National Intelligencer*, printed on the event:

Wend you with the world to-night?
　　Brown and fair, and wise and witty,
Eyes that float in seas of light,
　　Laughing mouths and dimples pretty,
Belles and matrons, maids and madams,
　　All are gone to Mrs. Adams'.

Mrs. Sullivan is there,
　　With all the charm that nature lent her;
Gay McKim, with city air;
　　And winning gales and Vandeventer;
Forsyth, with her group of graces;
　　Both the Crowninshields in blue;
The Pierces, with their heavenly faces,
　　And eyes like suns that dazzle through.
Belles and matrons, maids and madams,
　　All are gone to Mrs. Adams'.

Nor was Washington disappointed. The "Era of Good Feeling," as Monroe's presidency was termed, reached a brilliant climax in the ball which Louisa gave in her F Street home, and the city talked of the celebration long after the last candle had been snuffed, the last festoon of evergreen burned in the deep fireplace.

In the White House, which the Adamses entered in 1825, Louisa was as hospitable as she had been in the smaller home on F Street, although her failing health prevented her from entertaining as luxuriously as Dolley Madison had done. The cold, damp years in Russia had weakened Louisa. But, surrounded by the wives of cabinet members, she appeared at every official reception, welcoming guests to the White House.

In her last year as First Lady, she made a final gallant gesture. John had failed of re-election, and was hurt by the knowledge that the country which he had served so long and so loyally no longer wanted him for its leader. Andrew Jackson, after a bitter campaign, was to take his place as President of the United States. They were defeated, Louisa and John, but they would acknowledge it with their heads up; so Louisa arranged a last public reception at the White House. For the first time she did not surround herself with ladies of the cabinet and wait for guests to bow to her; instead, she moved about the audience room, greeting each guest personally, giving her hand to friends and political foes alike. Only John knew how tired she was, how disappointed for him.

Together they retired from the White House to their home on F Street. Although John, elected to Congress, again entered politics, public life was over for Louisa. After thirty-two years of it, she could again lose herself in her books and painting, in music and her garden, and she was happier in them than she had ever been in what she had once called "a life of change."

Rachel (Donelson) Robards Jackson

(1767–1828)

ZING!

"Look sharp, Rachel honey! Quick, down behind the gunwale," and Colonel John Donelson pulled his daughter with him to the bottom of the boat as he knelt and sighted his rifle to return the fire of hidden Indians.

Crouching quietly at his side like an obedient soldier, Rachel gripped the sail rope in her brown little hand, felt the line quiver as a Chickamauga bullet tore through the spread canvas, but only tightened her hold and deftly opened her father's powder horn, then his bullet pouch.

Just thirteen was Rachel, thirteen and clear-eyed, lithe as a young hunter, and equal to the wilderness, to its grim tangle of forest, its lurking Indians. Bullets winged over her head or cut into the side of the wooden boat with a splintering thud, but she steadily held the sail line and supplied lead shot to her father. As the strong current of the Tennessee River carried them farther and farther from the Indians, the sharp song of Chickamauga bullets dimmed to a whine, the spent leads dropped harmlessly into the water. Colonel Donelson, to save his stock of ammunition, ceased firing.

He rose, and at a nod from him Rachel, too, stood. Together they scanned the river behind them, taking a quick survey of the Harrison pirogue that followed in their wake. Harrison and his family seemed to be unhurt; yet Colonel Donelson hailed them rather anxiously, "Halloa-aa! All right there, Harrison?"

"Yes, Colonel. They never touched us, although one of their bullets smashed my best paddle," Harrison replied.

Donelson managed to smile, answering, "It's easier to patch a paddle than a man. Send the call down the line, will you?"

From boat to boat snapped the questioning "All right, there?" while Rachel and the Colonel waited for the halloo to reach the last of the fleet of forty. It seemed long to them, but it was only a moment or two until the call was relayed back to Harrison, who reported to his chief, "All right, Colonel, except Jonathan who got a flesh wound in the shoulder, and Stephens who has a crease across the head. None of the women or children was hurt."

Rachel saw her father's face relax at learning that none had been lost in the surprise attack. For more than two months—ever since they had sailed on December 22, 1779, from Fort Patrick Henry on the Holston River—the settlers had been in the care of Colonel Donelson. With a guard of thirty men he was leading one hundred and fifty women and children in a fleet of scows, canoes, and pirogues down the Tennessee River to the Cumberland to meet James Robertson and a group of men who had gone overland to establish the first white colony on the present site of Nashville.

Robertson and his men had started on their trek early in November of 1779. They had known they would have to fight their way through the hostile Indians who roamed

Kentucky, and believed their families, led by Donelson, would have a safer and easier journey on the river.

They did not realize, as they chopped and fought their way through Kentucky forests, that Donelson's little fleet was meeting dangers that equaled their own. Whirlpools shot several of the flimsy canoes onto jutting rocks, and even flung a heavily loaded scow upon the river bank. Once, three of the boats, including Colonel Donelson's, rammed onto Poor Valley Shoal. Again, the rushing current of the Tennessee drove a boat against a point of land, where it sank.

Bitterly cold winds and snow forced the entire fleet to tie up to land for almost a month. Food and ammunition became scarce, and Colonel Donelson ordered his followers to trap game in order to save the treasured powder and bullets. Rachel learned to set a snare for rabbits and to dig a pit, covered with brush, for a deer. When the men shot a bear and dragged the kill back into camp on a sled of branches, she helped render the fat for oil to be used in softening the hides and pelts that she and her mother made into skirts, blouses, and trousers.

In hastily built shelters, many sickened from exposure, and each day in the dreary camp added others to the sick list. At the first break in weather, Donelson ordered the company to break camp and cast off again on the voyage toward the Cumberland which none of them, not even Donelson, had ever seen.

Early in March they came upon fortified Indian villages, groups of mud and thatched huts set compactly at the river's edge. Although the voyagers carefully watched for movement in bushes and among trees on the bank, several surprise attacks were launched before they sighted the enemy. Even at night, when they made camp on shore, the company posted sentries and seized rifles whenever the dogs looked into the forest and barked restlessly.

By the time the fleet had reached the Cumberland there was no more food aboard the boats, so hunting parties were sent out to kill buffalo. Rachel, with several of the women, gathered herbs from river bottoms to make Shawnee salad; and the voyagers lived on herbs and the stringy meat of buffalo until April 24 when they landed at the Big Salt Lick, where Robertson and his men awaited them with supplies.

The long voyage was ended. The fight to make a home from the wilderness was begun.

Colonel Donelson led his family to a spring back in the timber and set to work at once, cutting, trimming and notching logs for a cabin. When the walls were laid in place and the ridgepole and purlins were roofed, Rachel and her mother chinked the logs with moss and mud to calk the cabin tight against rain and wind. They set their cooking crane up in the fireplace, stood a spinning wheel nearby, and spread a buffalo skin on the puncheon floor.

When the hickory fire blazed in the stout, wide fireplace and its light glanced off pewter mugs and plates on the table, there was a snug air of security in the little frontier cabin, a feeling of home, and the Donelsons smiled quietly at one another in the firelight. Sound walls stood between them and the wilderness, between them and the Indians. Outside those walls, they had to carry guns and be on constant guard.

Even while working in the garden Rachel heeded the faintest stir of leaves, the sudden chatter of birds startled by the approach of a human being. As she drove the cattle home from the canebrake pasturage, she watched the ground for the sign of an Indian raider—the print of a moccasin making a straight line in the earth. Only an Indian made straight moccasin prints, for, unlike a white man, he toed to neither right nor left as he swung along.

Neither Indians nor wilderness could discourage settlers from entering the fertile Tennessee territory. Scores of newcomers joined the Robertson colony on the Cumberland. The older settlers helped immigrants build cabins and start crops. While men felled timber and held log raisings, women met at one of the cabins, often at the Donelsons', to make quilts and deerskin clothes for the newcomers. At dusk the men trooped in for supper, then someone would catch up his fiddle, strike up "Hie Bettie Martin," and summon "all hands for a square-set."

Rachel, firelight glowing on her cheeks, her eyes brightly gay, laughed and swung into the middle of the floor with young Jeb Trubee as her partner. Jaunty in her soft buckskin skirt and blouse, she curtsied and retreated, caught her partner's hand and glided through measured steps as the genial fiddler called the numbers and zestfully played folk tunes the settlers had brought with them from "back home."

She was happy in the wilderness. She had courage and strength and the ability to adapt herself to the discipline and demands of the frontier, but she looked forward to visiting the "settlements" in Kentucky when Colonel Donelson decided to take his family there. They had not been there long before Rachel met Lewis Robards, whom she married after a brief courtship. The frontier girl and the somewhat spoiled, moody Robards were not suited to each other, and they separated. There was a reconciliation, but Rachel finally returned to her family who had gone back to Nashville.

It was an older, rather broken Rachel who returned to Nashville. She was still lithe and dark haired, but her eyes were a little deadened and her laugh a little slower.

It was this Rachel that Andrew Jackson found when he swirled in a gallop up to the Donelson house, in 1788, to ask for a room. Tall and thin-faced, with blue eyes that seemed almost to blaze, a saber cut streaking his forehead, Andrew Jackson was a stormy young frontier lawyer of twenty-one. He had been sent out to Tennessee to serve as public prosecutor, and he lunged into his task with a vigor which startled even the rugged frontiersmen. He was hard riding and hard fighting, and they admired him; he was impetuous and fearless, and they respected him.

In his companionship Rachel forgot much of the unhappiness that Kentucky had given her, and when they were married in 1791 she was once more the dashing, vivid Rachel who had danced at quilting parties. They built their home, Hunter's Hill, a few miles above Nashville, and smiled merrily at the Kents, the Hammonds, the Grays, and all of the rest who rode out to see "Andrew Jackson's board house." Most of Nashville saddled its horses, handed its ladies up to the pillion cushions, and trotted up the rutted clay road to admire Hunter's Hill, a frame house standing elegantly distinguished in a countryside of log cabins.

Rachel became the mistress of not only the house, but the plantation fields as well. Jackson's law cases kept him busy riding circuit; so Rachel superintended the farm work. When Jackson swung out of the plantation road, early in the morning, Rachel slipped into her homespun jacket, tied a sunbonnet snugly over her black hair, and mounted her own horse to canter smoothly off to the cotton and corn fields.

There was always a hearty "Good mawnin'!" for her from the field hands, and they grinned widely for they liked "Mis' Rachel," and worked even better for her than for Jackson, who was a natural leader of men.

Under her careful, patient supervision, Hunter's Hill prospered; its crops and its herds made it one of the leading plantations of Tennessee. But "Mis' Rachel," her throat and hands browned and windburned from her day in the fields, was always ready for a dance or a story when Jackson returned home to her. First, he laid aside the pistols that he carried in bearskin holsters, strapped to the pommel of his saddle; then pulled off his jack boots and tailed riding coat to get comfortable in moccasins and jacket. Supper was next, and then the evening before the fire, with Rachel lighting his long-stemmed clay pipe from a glowing hickory splinter, telling him of the day's work, how the hands had girdled the towering oak over in the east section, had cut those four sapling ash near the boundary line and cleared the patch for corn. Nor was her report entirely an account of what land had been cleared, what horses had been bought, what cattle had been driven into Nashville for sale. She noted humorous little incidents that took place in the daily life of the plantation, and related them to Jackson with the pungent, graphic humor of the frontier storyteller.

"And then I suppose you let old Zeke finish out his nap when you discovered him resting so gentle-like in the shade," commented Jackson, slapping his thin knees in great humor as Rachel told him of the truant who had snatched forty winks when he was supposed to have been hoeing corn.

"Well, yes, Andrew," Rachel answered, rather reluctantly; then added, twinkling, "he did look so peaceful, his kerchief over his face and his hands folded, that I just let him sleep a mite longer, then sent Job to wake him up, and he really worked twice as hard the rest of the day."

Hunter's Hill prospered, but Jackson lost his fortune in a collapse of the commercial paper of the day. He was forced to sell the proud "board house" and the land that Rachel had turned into richly bearing fields of grain and cotton. They began again, in a nearby log cabin which they called "The Hermitage," and once more Rachel took up the work of making a plantation. While Jackson, as Chief Justice of Tennessee, continued the public career that he had begun in his terms as United States Representative and Senator from the state, Rachel worked The Hermitage until it equaled the estate at Hunter's Hill.

Although The Hermitage was ten miles from Nashville, Rachel occasionally accompanied Jackson into town, and she never missed the gala Fourth of July celebration when the whole countryside gathered there for a barbecue and a program of races, speeches, and dancing. Even as the first rider slid from his saddle and tethered his horse, the tang of roasting meats—shotes and mutton and beef—browning over hickory coals drifted from wood fires that lined the center of a grove at the edge of Nashville.

By the time Rachel arrived, bringing a basket crowded with corn bread, tarts, pies, and cakes, tables had been set up, and men were lugging buckets of water from the cool spring. About midmorning, a fife and drum corps led the town's company of brightly uniformed volunteers into the grove, and, with sparkling eyes, Jackson watched the military drill, taking a salute from the captain. The volunteers had scarcely finished their last mimic charge when Holden James sounded his horn for the start of the foot races. Jackson tightened as he watched the young men crouch, taut, on the line, waiting for the gun signal. Rachel knew he was remembering the young days when he, too, had waited "at ready" on the mark, flung forward at the starting signal, and winged down the stretch to outrun them all.

She was glad when Holden, the races finished, called, "All right, now. Every man up for the shoot. We're going to fire from forty paces, at that ring on the big oak there."

Jackson was one of the first to draw from the hatful of turkey feathers which Holden proffered to the contestants. Drawing one that had a single notch on the quill, he opened the match. Rachel, holding his coat and neckcloth, smiled at his eager confidence as he settled the rifle into his lean shoulder, laid his cheek against the stock, and steadied himself for a quick, sure aim. Three times he sent leads dead into the heart of the ring on the oak. His days of wrestling and foot racing were over, but he was still a match for the best marksmen on the frontier, the hunters and scouts of Tennessee.

When Jackson volunteered his services for the War of 1812 and mustered in a company, scores of those same frontiersmen, clad in buckskin, moccasins, and coonskin caps, trekked in to enlist under his command. They followed him into the Indian country where they defeated the Creeks; they followed him to New Orleans and defeated the British; and they cheered him when, two years later, he invaded the Seminole country in Florida and captured Pensacola. "Old Hickory" was a frontiersman, a hard-riding and quick-shooting frontiersman who lived and fought in homespun. His was high courage and strength, and he held the loyalty of the frontiersmen who fought under his command and the loyalty of a frontierswoman, Rachel, who worked at The

Hermitage while he was charging into battle lines; who nursed him when he returned home, sick and worn with pain and fever.

Together, on his return from the Seminole War, they planned a new Hermitage, and were established in the white, pillared house when Jackson was elected United States Senator from Tennessee. Rachel accompanied him to Washington, but soon fled the scurrying, cramped life of the capital to return to Tennessee. Rachel, who had never flinched at Indian fire nor feared to ride a wilderness trail, had beaten a retreat from Washington and its social "attack" of luncheons, teas, formal dinners, and fifty calls a day. And yet, as mistress of The Hermitage, she was noted throughout Tennessee for her hospitality. Even with the General away in Washington, the plantation home was filled with guests, friends from Nashville, visiting soldiers and statesmen, friends of young Andrew Jackson Donelson and Andrew Jackson, Jr., Rachel's nephews who lived at The Hermitage.

She had made her retreat not so much from the people of Washington as from the city itself, hurrying back to wide, cotton-white plantation fields, to the forest, and the broad, calm river. Like Jackson, she was of the frontier; her life and her happiness were there in its freedom. It was almost with regret that she accepted the news of Jackson's election to the presidency in the autumn of 1828; and when a friend congratulated her, she was very grave in her answer, "For Mr. Jackson's sake, I am glad; for my own part, I never wished it."

That was in November. In a few months, she was to have entered a coach with Jackson for the journey to Washington and the White House, to become First Lady of the

Land. But Rachel did not go to the White House, did not leave the Tennessee she loved, for early in December she suffered a heart attack, and on December 22 the First Lady of the Frontier was dead.

Neither the honor of the White House nor the power of the presidency could compensate Jackson for her death. He gave her place as First Lady to "Lovely Emily," young wife of Rachel's nephew Andrew Jackson Donelson; but on Inauguration Day his eyes were bright with pain and loneliness, and he went into the White House a gaunt old man with memories of a laughing girl in homespun.

Hannah Hoes Van Buren

(1783–1819)

SLOWLY the grains of sand drifted through the slim neck of the hourglass and into a conelike heap at the bottom. Hannah forgot the sewing that was pinned to her skirt as she watched the trickle of sand in the glass and wondered if an hour could really be so long. Across the room the logs crackled in a dancing blaze; outside, a boisterous wind spattered snow against the windows; but the sand in the hourglass fell slowly, sleepily.

Suddenly Hannah felt the willow rod flick her shoulder.

"Mistress Hannah, what is it that takes your thought from your sewing so that you pay attention to nothing but the hourglass?" questioned Vrouw Lange, placing the long willow stick against the wall. There was no sound from the other pupils as they sewed busily, intent on hearing their schoolmate's answer. They knew that, no matter what she had been thinking of, Hannah Hoes would tell the truth.

"Well, Mistress Hannah?" and Vrouw Lange tapped her slipper on the brass foot warmer.

"It was only that I was wishing the sand would fall faster, because there is so much to do on St. Nicholas Eve, *goede vrouw.*"

Vrouw Lange nodded, smiled with the good humor that made hers the favorite dame school in the village, then rose from her mat chair as she said, "Yes, the hours seem long when one waits for St. Nicholas and his white horse, and," she added with a twinkle, "wonders if the good saint will leave toys and sweetmeats or a bundle of switches."

At the mention of switches—the gift made by St. Nicholas to children who had not been good throughout the year —Hannah's clear cheeks grew warm, and a blush rose to her curling golden hair. It was true that she had not been paying attention to Vrouw Lange, but it was so hard to think of anything other than St. Nicholas Eve, the opening of the Christmas season which began on December 5 and lasted through New Year's Day.

She twisted her slender hands in the folds of her woolen skirt for a moment, then looked up at Vrouw Lange. Before she could say anything, the schoolmistress comforted her with, "There will be no switches for you, Jannetje," addressing Hannah by the Dutch familiar name. "Nor for any of my scholars. You have all been very good this year, and now I have a surprise for you that I was going to keep until the end of the hour. Come, Jannetje, help me with the tray."

Vrouw Lange crossed the room to the high walnut cupboard, and with Hannah carried a pewter dish of *klaasjes* to the hearth. Although there were only nine scholars, dozens of St. Nicholas cakes cut in the shapes of lambs, ducks, fish, and birds heaped the tray. On a smaller plate Vrouw Lange had placed neat little rows of marchpane, almond paste molded into pink hearts and snowy turtledoves.

Of all the women in Kinderhook, the New York village on the Hudson River, she best remembered the folk cus-

toms of the motherland. All of Kinderhook had roast goose
and chestnuts on St. Martin's Day, *klaasjes* and letter cakes
on St. Nicholas Eve; cut green branches at Pinkster, and
eagerly took part in the market-day fun of the Kermis; but
Jannetje and her friends went to Vrouw Lange when they
wanted to hear of the pranks played by the masked children
of Holland on Shrove Tuesday, the merry pageant of May
Day, the candle jumping on Twelfth Night.

They had just finished an old Dutch Christmas song
when Vrouw Lange warned, "Hurry now, get into your
jackets and shawls and hurry home, or you will be late for
the *koek-plakken*."

Hannah was the first to the door. Snow swirled around
her as she stepped from the stoop and looked about the
yard. Sighting a dark figure flinging its arms and stamping
its feet, she laughed and ran toward it, calling, "Oh, I'm
sorry, Martin, to have made you wait. Are you really very
cold?"

His long eyelashes were wet with snow, and his knitted
cap, pulled tightly over his bright hair, was caked white with
little patches of ice; but he grinned and caught Hannah's
school bag as he answered, "I'm so cold that you will have
to do my share of the cake pasting while I sit in the stew
kettle to get thawed."

Martin Van Buren's voice was low but full of energy. At
thirteen he was slender but firmly built; his forehead was
high, and his eyes, blue like Hannah's, were deep-set; his
mouth was wide and sharply curved.

All their lives, Hannah and he had been playmates. During the school months, he rose early to finish his tasks at
the Van Buren tavern in time to accompany her to Vrouw
Lange's, continuing on to his classes at the academy for the

boys of Kinderhook. Together they walked home past the steepled church, past the neat little shops with sanded floors, the village green where garlanded booths were set up each year for the Kermis.

On holidays, they trudged through the snow to the coasting hill; or, bright scarfs whipping round their faces, skated doggedly into the wind and swooped into long gliding figure eights and frosty circles, their curved iron skates ripping little furrows in the ice. In the mellow, sunlit days of summer they played on the green, Hannah rolling a hoop or turning a jump rope while Martin knuckled down at marbles with his schoolmates, shot with bow and arrow, or batted the horsehair ball in *kaetzen*. November brought St. Martin's Day, and they built flaring bonfires, "St. Martin's fires," and scuttled little iron baskets of chestnuts back and forth over the flames.

By the time they reached home, Vrouw Hoes had placed several lengths of thin cake upon the kitchen table. Hannah was already getting strips of gold and silver paper from the cupboard as Dirk, Jacob, Gertrude, and Anna arrived from their houses to take part. When they had decorated the cakes until they shone like pieces of treasure, supper was ready for them: pea porridge, venison, currant bread, waffle cakes, and cheese. They ended the evening with dancing and St. Nicholas songs.

School ended in late spring, but it seemed to Hannah that the summer holiday was over almost before it had really begun. Classes started again, and she went to them alone, for Martin had been taken out of school and articled to be a lawyer. Vrouw Van Buren had wanted to keep him at his studies but could no longer afford to; so he clerked in a store during the day and read for the law at night. He

was only fifteen when he summed up his first case, climb-
ing on a chair so the court could see him while he spoke.

As he steadily advanced to recognition among the lawyers
of the state, he became interested in politics. By 1807 he
was a leader in county politics and a successful lawyer with
an established income; so, one morning in February of that
year, he tucked Hannah into a sleigh and drove her to the
neighboring village of Catskill, where they were married.

For twelve years Hannah watched him work toward a
command of New York politics, and knew his love of the
turmoil and battle, even while he told her that he wished
he could desert the field and devote himself to law. She saw
him advance in public office, but she did not live to see him
gain the presidency of the United States.

Martin Van Buren gave Hannah's place as hostess to no
one until his son, Major Abraham Van Buren, brought a
bride to the White House, Angelica Singleton Van Buren,
daughter of a South Carolina planter and a niece of Dolley
Madison.

Martin Van Buren had won the triumph that Hannah
had wanted for him when she realized—in that village on
the Hudson—his ambition for leadership.

Anna Symmes Harrison
(1775–1864)

"WELL, Lieutenant Harrison, I understand you have married my daughter." The voice of Judge John Cleve Symmes was even more chilled and hostile than it had been on the day he forbade the marriage. "You waited until I was called away on business, then you had the effrontery to be married in my own house!"

"It was the only thing we could do, Judge Symmes," Harrison answered quietly. "Anna and I love each other; and the slanderous things you have heard about me and hold against me are not true; but you would not believe me when I told you they were false. I have done nothing wrong in marrying Anna."

The older man wondered if he had been unfair in condemning on hearsay a man whom he knew to be a gallant soldier, but he was not yet reconciled to the marriage; so he asked, bluntly, "And how do you expect to support her?"

"With my sword and my right arm!" answered Harrison.

The judge had also been a soldier, serving as captain in the Continental Army, and the spirited independence of his new son-in-law pleased him. "With your sword and your right arm, eh? I believe you will take care of Anna all right. But, come we had better join the others at table."

Officers who had gathered at Fort Washington for the dinner honoring "Mad Anthony" Wayne smiled, as they watched the two men cross the candlelighted mess room arm in arm, and they said to one another, "Harrison is a winner in love as well as in war. No one can stay angry with him long."

"Mad Anthony" was the guest of honor, but he arose, lifted his glass, and called: "Gentlemen, a toast! A toast to the fairest bride in Northwest Territory, Anna Symmes Harrison!"

Led by the general, officers of the garrison gave the toast with enthusiasm, for Anna was a noted beauty. After the Revolution she had gone with her father from their Long Island home and settled at North Bend, Ohio. As their cabin was just a few miles from Cincinnati, the location of Fort Washington, it became a favorite gathering place for officers of the post; but when Lieutenant William Henry Harrison arrived at the fort from Virginia it was he who became Anna's favorite partner.

Although he was appointed commander of Fort Washington soon after his marriage, he resigned his commission to enter politics. Both Anna and he welcomed his appointment by President John Adams to the office of Territorial Secretary; but Anna was even more delighted when Harrison was called to appear before Congress in Philadelphia. Not only was her husband started on his public career but they were to visit together the national capital, the gayest city in America.

She knew the journey would be long and hard, yet with a sort of holiday feeling she packed the few clothes she could carry in a saddlebag and mounted her horse. Harrison led the way as they rode the clay trails, splashed through fords, explored grass-tufted swamps, and bent over their saddles to avoid branches over forest paths.

Toward the end of the day they would look for a cabin where they could put up for the night. First there would be the challenging bark of a hunting dog, then a thin blue twist of wood smoke and the sight of a log cabin standing rough and square in the center of a cleared patch. No matter who was the owner, they knew he would give them food and lodging for the night. That was the way in frontier country.

"Hallo-aa, the house!" called Harrison as he and Anna rode into the clearing; but the owner, warned by his dog, was already standing in the doorway, rifle in hand. "Can you put us up for the night, friend?"

"Can't offer you much, but glad to share it with you," answered the settler. "Here, I'll take your horses," and he slipped his arm through the rawhide bridles.

Peck's cabin was scantily furnished with a plank table and bench that he had hewn and pegged from timber cleared off his land, two squat three-legged stools, and a trundle bed on hand-adzed rockers. Hanging from one wall were a skillet and half a dozen gourd spoons and jars; a corner of the windowless cabin was cheered by a blue and white Carolina coverlet, which covered a shuck bed. Over the door, resting on prongs of twisted antlers, was Peck's deer rifle. A hand mill of stone already stained by crushed corn stood next to Mrs. Peck's spinning wheel near the fireplace.

"We haven't been here long, and the Injuns have been mighty pesky; that's why I keep open those peepholes in the walls," Peck explained. "But we're getting on all right, and I can set in more corn next spring and maybe hunt enough this winter to take some pelts down to Cincinnati. Mary here has learned to handle a gun as good as I can, and she says she can take care of herself and the baby while I'm gone. Still, I don't like what happened up at Wright's place the other day while Jim Wright was down at the fort."

While Peck told Harrison of the Indian raid on the Wright cabin, the women roasted venison hams and baked corn dough into johnnycakes. After dinner, Anna and Harrison wrapped themselves in their riding cloaks and slept on the floor, their booted feet near glowing embers of the fire.

Once or twice on the journey they failed to find shelter; then they had to make camp for the night in the forest. While Harrison unsaddled the horses, Anna took his hunting knife and searched for dry twigs and scraped the punk-like heart of a rotting tree into her hand. When she returned with the tinder, she built it into a tiny tepee. She knelt with her cloak spread wide to shelter it from any wind, while Harrison struck his steel and flint and blew a wavering sleepy flame from it, gradually building a steady blaze by feeding the little quaver of fire with birch that he had cut.

Taking a burning twig, they made four other little fires to dry the ground on which they were to sleep, then gathered a few handfuls of acorns which they roasted and pounded between two stones. Anna patted the acorn meal into little cakes and wrapped them in wet leaves which she buried in the hot ashes of a fire. They made their supper of the ash cakes and pemmican, which Harrison always carried in his saddlebag, drank from a nearby creek with cupped hands, then cleared away the four drying fires and went to sleep on the few branches they had heaped on the ground. Once during the night, Harrison wakened to replenish the fire, their only guard against wolves they heard howling in the timber.

Midway in Pennsylvania they came to the beginning of a stage line that would take them into Philadelphia; so they sold their horses and completed the journey in coaches.

Travel by stage was faster and more comfortable than travel by horseback, but Anna was glad when they reached Philadelphia and the Spread Eagle.

Although the capital lacked the social leadership of a First Lady, as Abigail Adams was ill on her Braintree farm, it was gay with assemblies and dinners. When Anna returned to her frontier home at the end of the winter, she carried with her memories of afternoons spent in the gabled brick houses of Philadelphia where candles burned in silver sconces and tea was served in fragile porcelain cups, where polished mahogany and black walnut furniture gleamed. It was all very different from her home on the frontier, but the return to the wilderness meant that Harrison had made another advance in his career, for President Adams had appointed him Governor of the Territory of Indiana with headquarters at Vincennes.

Harrison bought a large tract of land just north of Vincennes, the oldest settlement in Indiana, and built a brick house somewhat in the style of those in Philadelphia. The Harrison home, Grouseland, became the center of social and official life in the Territory. Men in fringed deerskin hunting clothes, women in skirts and jackets woven from flax and buffalo hair journeyed to Grouseland for hoe downs.

As Harrison was in charge of Indian affairs, chiefs of the Delawares, Munsees, and Piankeshaws were frequent visitors. They beached their bark canoes near the curve in the river where Anna set flax to soak, and stalked up to Grouse-land. When the powerful Shawnee, Tecumseh, led his warriors up from the Wabash to confer with Harrison on land purchases, Anna seated herself at one corner of the veranda to observe the council.

More than any other man, Tecumseh had worked to better the condition of the Indians. He urged them to meet the aggressiveness of the white man with their own strength, and tried to teach them that they must each hold a piece of ground and sow and harvest it.

Over Tecumseh's protest, Harrison continued to treat with individual tribes and buy land from them, following President Jefferson's policy of opening the country for the whites. Tecumseh, still determined to band the Indians together, had come to Grouseland to tell Harrison again that he must buy land only when all the tribes agreed.

Tall and rugged, he strode up to the Governor, lifted his hand with palm outward, and saluted him with a grave, "Brother, we come in the name of all the tribes. We come, Brother, that you may give us justice."

While the council fire was being lighted on the ground before the house, warriors seated themselves. Their blankets were wrapped about them, and their guns and bows lay near them. Harrison kept his hands at his side, away from his sword; but Anna felt again for the small hunting knife she had tucked beneath her dress. She knew how swiftly those impassive, blanketed braves could leap up to attack him, and she wanted her knife ready. The militia which Harrison had called to stand guard at Grouseland seemed scant as it faced the great circle of armed Indians.

While she looked out at the braves seated on the grass, their faces streaked with vermilion and ocher clay, throats encircled by necklaces of bear claws, hair twisted about red and green and yellow feathers, she heard Harrison again explain his position to Tecumseh. The settlers had come, he said, but the Government was willing to pay for the land they took.

But as her husband spoke, Anna saw Tecumseh's mouth tighten at the words he had heard before, the words that seemed to goad him into anger and defiance.

Her fingers gripped the hunting knife. Still Harrison kept his hands at his sides; but at a quick move and a harsh mutter from the Shawnee his manner suddenly changed from that of peacemaker to that of challenger. He abruptly asked the interpreter, "What did Tecumseh say then?"

The interpreter kept his eyes on the glowering Shawnee as he answered Harrison, "He said that you spoke false things. He said you lied."

Anna tried to run to her husband's side but was held back by a lieutenant of the guard. Then she heard Harrison's voice, hard and peremptory, "Put out the council fire. I will talk no longer with Tecumseh who came here as a guest and made himself a foe. Put out the council fire, I say!"

That evening Harrison wrote to President Madison of the crisis which Tecumseh had created. When Anna brought him sand with which to blot the letter, he studied the dispatch anxiously, and said, "I am afraid that there can be no peace until we have broken the power of Tecumseh. . . ."

For a year, however, Harrison worked to keep peace; then, in November of 1811, he was ordered to protect the pioneers by a military expedition, and he led his men to defeat the Indians at Tippecanoe, winning Indiana for the settlers.

Post riders carried news of the victory to Washington and New York, Philadelphia, and Boston, and Harrison was talked of everywhere—Harrison and Tippecanoe. Years later, when Harrison ran against Martin Van Buren, with John Tyler for Vice-President, the public still thought of the general as the victor at Tippecanoe. In what became the most spectacular of all presidential campaigns, the slogan was "Tippecanoe and Tyler too."

For the greater part of that hearty, roistering campaign Anna was ill and unable to accompany Harrison on his speaking tours. But even at North Bend—where they had moved from Vincennes—she heard "Tippecanoe and Tyler too." The villagers paraded through the streets ringing bells, carrying torches, shouting their praise of the veteran General.

Like Harrison partisans throughout the country, they built log cabins which symbolized the General's life on the old frontier; they flew flags and banners from houses; staged parades in which brightly colored floats carried dugout canoes, log cabins, caged raccoons, and 'possums. As they marched they sang:

> For Tippecanoe and Tyler too—Tippecanoe
>   and Tyler too;
> And with them we'll beat little Van;
> Van, Van, Van is a used-up man;
> And with them we'll beat little Van.

They sang and they marched; they paraded and shouted; and Anna smiled at their excitement and at Harrison's enthusiasm. For years she had known his ambition to become President, and he had waited long for the honor.

When neighbors gathered to celebrate Harrison's election, she was well enough to go out on the porch for a moment to listen to cheers for the General, now the President-elect. She saw him, dark against the flaring red of torches, raise his hand in a military salute, then bow.

She hoped to be able to accompany him to Washington for his inauguration, but she was not strong enough to travel then, planning to start for the White House a few weeks later. She did not see her husband as President of the United States, for word of his death came early in April, just as she was preparing to begin her Washington journey.

The young officer who had promised to support her with his sword and right arm was gone—and with him had gone the frontier as Anna had known it, when smokes from council fires had wreathed the trees before their home.

Letitia Christian Tyler

(1790–1842)

VERY fresh and cool against her hand was the rose that Asa, the table boy, had laid beside her breakfast plate. The half-opened petals, so richly dark that they were almost crimson, and the firm pointed leaves still held flecks of dew. As she lifted the rose to catch its fragrance, Letitia studied it for a moment. Then quickly she replaced it on the table, and smiled.

"What is it, Mother?" asked John, who was sitting next to her. "What made you smile that way?"

"What way, son?" Letitia's quiet voice was somewhat hurried, as though John's question interested her unusually.

"Well, Mother, if Letty had smiled so," nodding across the table to his sister, "I should have known she was thinking up some new mischief. But you never do plan mischief; so I just wondered what that funny little quirk did mean. Have you a surprise for us? Is Father coming home from Washington? Is that it?"

Letitia motioned to Asa to put another wheat cake on John's plate, then answered, "Perhaps I was planning mischief, son; but I really did not consider it very seriously. No, Father will not be home until the end of Congress; and, by the way, John, you and Letty must write to him tonight."

When breakfast was finished, Letitia picked up the rose and carried it with her to the veranda where she stood for an instant, looking out over the garden. It was spring in tidewater Virginia, and the faint wind of early morning was a drift of fragrance from the wild roses in the woods, the peach blossoms in the orchard, the sweetbrier in the lanes. It was spring in tidewater Virginia: the sky was very blue, the cloud puffs very white; and Letitia, with the rose still in her hand, thought of the "mischief" which had tempted her. She had lived all of her life in Virginia, but the Southern springtime still enchanted her.

"Just one day in which to play truant!" she said softly to herself. "Just one day in which I could sit in the garden and watch the roses, or walk in the woods and do nothing. One day. But," she reminded herself, "as John says, I don't plan 'mischief.' "

Quickly, she turned and entered the house, going to her desk where she knew that Robertson, the overseer, awaited her inspection of the plantation accounts. Ever since her marriage in 1813 to the brilliant Virginia statesman, John Tyler, Letitia had superintended the plantation so that her husband could be free to serve in public office. His career had been unusually successful, but the government salaries were small; so, like Abigail Adams, Letitia devoted herself to farming. She could help her husband in that way, and there were not many days when she wanted to desert her work.

Even though the wide windows near her desk were open over the garden and the gentle wind sifted through them to stir her hair, Letitia forgot to wish to be a truant as she listened to Robertson's report.

Letitia, clever as well as lovely, managed the Tyler plantation.

"Very well, then, Mr. Robertson, I shall write today for an order of iron. Meanwhile, have Esau use what he has in the blacksmith shop to forge a new jack plow; and tell Samuel that he will have to finish repairing the wagons this week so that he can get started on making hogsheads." Letitia closed the ledger in which she had been writing notes during the overseer's report and carefully dried her quill pen. "Oh, yes, Mr. Robertson, one more thing. Excuse Molly from garden work for the rest of the day, and tell her to prepare the end cabin in the quarters for Junius and herself. They are to be married tomorrow, you know, and

that end cabin is in good repair; so Molly will find it easy
to get ready."

When Robertson had ridden back to the fields, Letitia
began her morning round, going first to the dairy where
four Negro girls worked under the direction of Aunt Becky,
a slave who had been at Greenway before John Tyler was
born. Nearby was the spinning and sewing house, where the
most skilled of the slave women fashioned dresses and
skirts for their "Missus" and "Young Missy" as well as
clothes for all of the Negroes at Greenway. There were
made the ruffled petticoats—two for each dress—the cotton
underclothes, puckered aprons, dresses with snug high
waists, flaring coats with tiny shoulder capes.

"I am just going to run through here this morning, Sally
Sue," Letitia greeted the head slave woman, " 'cause I want
to go into town right after dinner. Can you get that silk
dress finished for me this morning?"

After her brief but thorough inspection, Letitia visited
the cookhouse and was on her way to the garden when she
heard the tinkle of a peddler's bell on the gravel drive leading to the mansion house.

"Good day, ma'm. Pins, buttons, needles, scissors, shoes,
baskets, clocks. Pins, buttons, needles, scissors, shoes,
baskets, clocks—all of the best quality, ma'm, and at the
best prices. Truly a treasure, ma'm, truly a treasure." The
peddler continued his rapid singsong even as he climbed
down from the wagon and swooped his beaver hat in a wide
bow to the smiling mistress of Greenway. Before she could
answer he had grandly waved her to a chair on the veranda
and lifted a large box of pins and buttons from his wagon.

"The best that is made in Connecticut, ma'm, and
bought by the best plantations in Virginia. A treasure!"

Letitia consulted the notebook that hung at her wrist. Pins, buttons, and needles were needed in the sewing room.

For herself she selected a Philadelphia horn comb, ruddy and glistening from the long polishing it had been given in wood and ashes; then just one more purchase remained to be made, and she seemed to be quite particular about it. "I want a bright shawl, a very gay one; red would be best, I think. It is for a slave who is going to be married tomorrow." Together they chose Molly's wedding present, as the peddler gossiped about the news of the countryside, the prospects of a good tobacco crop, the boggy conditions of Southern roads, styles in bonnets.

As he was speaking, the dinner bell rang; so Letitia invited him to rest at Greenway during the noon hour, sending Asa out with a tray of food for the peddler to eat on the shaded veranda.

Soon after dinner, the coachman brought the phaeton to the door, and a groom stood at the head of the horses, steadying them with soothing strokes of his hands. Before she stepped into the carriage, Letitia noted that the phaeton was spotless and shining, the harness polished, the horses' coats curried and brushed to a sleek luster. She did not look at Jeb, the coachman, for she knew that in the pride of his position he had carefully sanded and brushed his tall beaver hat and scoured the brass buttons on his tailed coat.

After supper that night, Letitia sat in the garden with John and Letty. She talked but little, content to rest and listen to the chirrup of the field crickets. She only half heard the songs that came dimly from the slave quarters. At first she wondered why they were singing—no itinerant preacher had come to Greenway, and the slaves seldom held a group sing unless there were a celebration of some sort. Then she remembered that Molly and Junius were to be married the next day, and realized that all the slaves had gathered at the end cabin for a "jollification." Jeb, always the song leader, would be standing before the seated slaves who would wait until he started a verse, then catch the refrain from him and answer in a chorus.

The Negro voices lifted high, lifted sweet, Letitia began to drowse, strangely lulled by the spring night and the muted music.

Years later, long after she had said goodby to Virginia and had gone to Washington to become First Lady of the Land, she wistfully recalled that spring night in the garden at Greenway. So long ago, she thought, so very long ago; and her fingers tightened around the arm of her chair. She was ill, unable to leave her room, and she had given her place as First Lady to her daughter Letty, who presided at White House functions for President Tyler.

Although Letitia was not able to help John Tyler, she smiled happily every time she thought of him as "President Tyler," for she had helped him attain that office. He spent every moment he could in her room with her, telling her of his work. what he had seen, and the news of Washington; but when she was alone her thoughts went back to Virginia, often thinking of what John Tyler had said while courting her.

He had been very serious when he said it, but Letitia had smiled, and she still smiled when she remembered his words: he was glad that he was poor when he asked her to marry him, explaining that if he had been wealthy he should always have feared that she accepted him because of his fortune. Because she had accepted him when he was poor, he knew that it was because she loved him.

As Letitia's memory went back to those youthful days she found herself being glad, too, that they had been poor, that she had had the opportunity to help him to success. Throughout the year before her death at the White House that thought seemed almost to compensate for her illness —her husband was President of the United States, and she had helped to make him so.

Julia Gardiner Tyler
(1820–1889)

JULIA TYLER, twenty-four and sparkling with the excitement of being First Lady of the Land, paced back and forth across the dressing room as she pinned a diamond brooch to her evening gown. It was several months since she had become mistress of the White House, through her marriage to President Tyler on June 26, 1844.

Humming a wandering little tune, she chanced to stop by a window that opened toward a lot near the White House—her breath caught in her throat. She saw a crowd circled around a bonfire. Flames shot toward the sky. She heard derisive shouts, taunting laughter; and she shut her eyes tightly and flung back her head as though to shake away what she had seen. But she could still hear the mockery of the jeering crowd as it burned in effigy the "Veto President," her husband.

It was only for a moment that Julia clung to the window ledge, white and shaken. There was a knock at the door; so, quickly, she steadied herself and turned from the window. Opening the door, she found her husband waiting to take her to dinner.

"You are pale, Julia. What is the matter?" he asked, entering the room.

She only shook her head, knowing her voice would tremble should she try to speak. Before she could take his arm to get him out of the room, away from what she had seen, he smiled rather gravely and crossed to the window she had just left. Then, looking out toward the bonfire, he said very quietly, "Yes, I know, Julia. It isn't pleasant to see the President of the United States being burned in effigy, particularly if he happens to be your husband. I saw that fire from my study; that is why I hurried here to you.

"But, Julia," and he returned to her side and put his hand on her shoulder, "I have seen this before; and though it hurts just as much every time I do see it, the people can burn me in effigy all they want if they will just let me carry through my work on annexing Texas. If I can get Texas into the Union before I go out of office I shall be satisfied that my administration has been a success. Come, now, Julia, come with me down to dinner and let my effigy blaze away out there."

The bonfire had burned out by the time the first guests arrived at the White House that evening for President Tyler's reception, yet many of them had already heard of the humiliating episode. News, particularly scandalous news, traveled very fast in Washington. But as the guests filed into the Blue Room to greet—and to scrutinize—the President and Julia, not one was able to note if the couple knew of the effigy burning. Both John and Julia were as serene and hospitable as though they had only the most agreeable thoughts. John was courtly and charming. Julia was gracious and smiling.

Even before they had been married, Julia had known of the stormy administration through which John Tyler was struggling. As the daughter of Senator David Gardiner of New York, she had heard of Tyler's effort to control his Congress, but not until she became First Lady did she realize the stubborn, lone fight that the Virginian was making.

As the line of reception guests thinned for a moment, she managed to take a hurried look at her husband. Although he was still erect and his voice still firm in its persuasive resonance, his hair was whitening and his face thinning. Julia wondered if he found his fight worth while. Then she remembered what he had said about Texas, how his eyes had brightened.

As Tyler's administration neared its end, however, he began to win back some of the popularity which had attended him throughout most of his public life, and there were happier days in the Executive Mansion. He even achieved his ambition to annex Texas. On the last day he was in office, Congress passed resolutions to admit the Lone Star republic into the Union. When Julia left Washington on March 5, 1845, she carried away with her, as her most treasured memento, the gold pen with which her victorious husband had signed the Texas resolutions.

Julia, daughter of a senator, became the President's second wife.

Sarah Childress Polk

(1803–1891)

On that June afternoon of 1844 New York financiers gathered as usual in the crimson and gold lounge of the Astor House at the end of the business day in Wall Street. Their talk, however, was not the usual discussion of the excellent coffee they were sipping nor of the day's happenings on the Exchange. Just one question interested them— "Who is this man Polk?"

One ventured: "Oh, he is just some Southern nobody who has served a few terms in Congress. He doesn't stand a chance to get the election away from Henry Clay. 'Old Hal' will be our next President." At this the New Yorkers shook their heads, tapped their gold-topped, slender canes against their boots, and wondered what the country was coming to, that an unknown man should dare to run for the presidency.

All up and down the Atlantic coast, in grave Philadelphia and busy Boston, and throughout the Western territory, men asked one another, "Who is Polk?" then shook their heads and wondered what the country was coming to. But in the South, in Tennessee, men were saying, "We are going to give the Whigs a run for their money. James K.

Polk is a fighter. He doesn't say much, but he goes right along."

And yet, even while they spoke so confidently, their challenge was tinged with uneasiness. It was the first time in the history of the United States that an "unknown" had been named as a presidential candidate, and the South was not certain that it could vote him into the office which Washington and Jefferson and Madison had held. Until 1844 only men of fame had been nominated, and no one needed to ask, "Who is Jackson?" or "Who is Harrison?" but now almost everyone questioned, "Who is Polk?" And so the South whistled to keep up its spirits and bravely talked about what a good fighter James Polk was, and hoped for the best.

But there was one person in the South who had faith in the "unknown," and her faith in him was wholehearted. She had watched him plod his way from an obscure law practice in a small Tennessee town to a place in the state legislature, to Congress where he had served seven consecutive terms as a representative, to the governor's chair at Nashville. On that way there had been no spectacular marches, no flourishes; there had been just a steady, direct climb—and she had shared it with him, for Sarah and James Polk had shared everything in their lives. As a young lawyer, not long out of the University of North Carolina, James Polk had discussed his first cases with Sarah, and she had helped him formulate his pleas. Later, when he had advanced into state and national politics, he talked with her about legislative questions, and together they worked on speeches that he was to present.

After the first moment of surprise, at the news of Polk's nomination, Sarah was unstirred by the restless uncertainty

which pervaded the nation. Five months intervened between the nomination and the election, but Sarah immediately began helping in her husband's campaign, which for the most part was carried on from the Polk home in Columbia, Tennessee. All day long and into the night, under the hot oil lamps, Sarah and James studied and filed the campaign correspondence, wrote to the party leaders, outlined for the newspapers Polk's affirmative stand on the annexation of Texas. They worked as they had always done, quietly, doggedly, and thoroughly—together.

And when, in November, their work was finished, they had won, for James Polk had been elected President of the United States. With the sudden enthusiasm with which America greets each President-elect, the nation hailed Polk as its new champion. Not even on the inaugural journey to Washington, however—when crowds saluted the presidential party on the river docks at Cincinnati and Louisville—did the two make any flourishes.

Once in the White House, dark-eyed Sarah brought back the crystalline serenity which had been the tone of the Executive Mansion in the days of Elizabeth Kortright Monroe. The White House, the home of the chief representative of the United States of America, should be, Sarah felt, a place of dignity at all times, and so she stated that neither card playing nor dancing would be allowed there so long as she was First Lady. In spite of her edict, she became one of the most popular of White House hostesses. Although she still read and judged her husband's public speeches, discussed political problems and the cabinet's opinions with him, she found time in which to hold two evening receptions each week, to give state dinners, and arrange for informal parties throughout the winter season.

She particularly pleased the President by holding a reception each Saturday morning that Congress was in session. He not only disliked social activity but was reluctant to take time from his work to meet visitors to the White House; so Sarah made friends for them both, meeting the Representatives and Senators every Saturday. Some of them knew that their hostess was as well informed about politics as they, yet she never spoke on that subject. She kept her own counsel until the time when she and her husband would sit at the hearth in her parlor and talk over his plans. Sometimes, when the cabinet disagreed with Polk's opinions, she too disagreed and was firm in her disapproval.

Of one thing they talked but little, even though it was Sarah's chief concern. Toward the end of his administration Polk was tiring, his health visibly breaking. He had gone into office at fifty as one of the youngest Presidents; but he insisted upon being the sole leader of his administration, and the toil had drained his strength.

Before he retired from office, he bought a home in Nashville, a two-story house set in deep shrub-filled grounds, which he called the "Polk Place." As Sarah watched her husband in the last few months at the White House, saw his face losing color, his hands thinning, she was eager for the time when he could return to the South and rest in his new home.

She was almost impatient of the pageantry and demonstrative admiration with which every town greeted Polk as he journeyed home from Washington. No one was more proud of James Polk than she, but she feared the effect that the excitement and the delays might have on his failing health.

Her anxiety was justified, for he had been home only a

few weeks when he succumbed to a fever that ended in death. Left alone in her new home, Sarah tried to continue as she had when James had been there. His law books still lined the large room off the hall which he had used as a study in the short time before his death; his manuscripts lay on the writing table; a letter rested near the lamp. When the Nashville guards paraded to the Polk Place, marching under the arched trees to the house, Sarah reviewed them from the porch. At the end of their drill the guards presented arms as their tribute of honor to her. Tall, her dark hair whitening, her head proudly erect, she accepted that salute as a tribute not to herself, but to her husband, once President of the United States of America.

Margaret Smith Taylor

(1788–1852)

WHEN the last tent had been struck and stowed away in Number 3 wagon, the last side of bacon and sack of beans rolled into the commissary chest, the dragoons of Colonel Zachary Taylor's command belted on their cartridge boxes and slung their rifles into carrying position, ready for marching orders.

As they swung into line, four abreast in the twisting wilderness road, their colonel passed them on his way back to the wagon train. At his side was a small merry person bundled in an army greatcoat. One brown hand thrust its way out of the long crumpled sleeve to lift a trailing skirt from the ground, the other hand was tucked under the colonel's arm; and the clear light voice was saying, "And when we get to Fort Crawford I'm going to make you stay in bed until you get over this cold. Thank goodness, I'll soon have you out of a tent and into a cabin."

Zachary Taylor, veteran of the War of 1812, smiled as he swung his wife into her place in Number 1 wagon, saying, "Yes, Mrs. Colonel, when we get to the fort I'll take your orders for a while; but, right now, you are under my orders. From what the scouts tell me I don't expect any more trouble from the redskins on the rest of the journey; but if we do have a brush I want you to promise me, Margaret, that you will drop to the floor of the wagon at the first rifle shot and stay there until I come back for you. And, Margaret, keep your powder dry."

Often as she had heard his warning to "keep her powder dry," she never failed to smile an assurance that she would and then to delve into the huge square pocket of her army coat to bring out the pistol so he could inspect its priming. Corporal McRae, her driver, sometimes wondered why Margaret did not impatiently answer the Colonel that she could really remember so simple a warning from day to day; but Margaret knew what Corporal McRae did not know, that the words were more than an admonition. They were Zachary's way of making her his partner for all of the long day on the march. And so, each time that she heard them, she nodded and smiled back her answer.

She had scarcely settled herself amid the gear on the wagon floor and pulled the buffalo robe round her booted feet when the order, "Company! Forward march!" went down the line and the column briskly set off into the north toward Fort Crawford at Prairie du Chien, Wisconsin. Bracing herself against the worn oak chest which held all of the Colonel's and her clothes and their camp kit, she began her day of mending and knitting while Corporal McRae occasionally turned sideways on the driving box to tell her of the latest mess news or to ask if she would write a letter home for him—knowing that she would.

For more than twenty years Margaret Taylor had shared the frontier life of her soldier husband, making tent and log cabin into home for him. Once, soon after their marriage in 1810, he had prevailed upon her to stay with his people in Kentucky while he went out to the Indiana Territory to serve as commander of Fort Harrison. On his return he found a bride who was determined not to be separated again from him; so he gladly took her with him on the rest of his assignments and campaigns.

Together they broke trail on the frontier, lived warily in small stockaded outposts, cut off from all the comforts and amusements of "back home," yet neither of them complained. Taylor had been a soldier since boyhood and his whole interest lay in the army. Margaret, who had not had the hard frontier training of her husband reared in pioneer Kentucky, schooled herself to the rigorous demands of wilderness life.

As soon as her children were old enough to leave her, however, she sent them back to the Taylors in Kentucky or to her people in Maryland, to be educated. So long as Zachary was kept on the frontier she would stay with him, but their children must go to school and learn the ways of the people back home. Whenever Sarah or Betty or Dick teased to stay with their father and mother in the wilderness, Zachary would try to look very stern and then order them to their "posts." Often, while Margaret and he were crouched at a fire before their tent, he would look up from the letter he was writing to one of the children and say with a certain stubborn solemnity: "Our girls are not going to marry into the army. You and I are old campaigners, Margaret, and we know what it's like. It's all right for you and me, because we can take care of ourselves; but I won't have it for Sarah and Betty."

Wilderness marches were hard; garrison life was monotonous, constricted; the homeless living in tents, cabins, and gaunt wagons was a meager sort of living. Zachary and

Margaret would not have it for their children; but Zachary, the soldier, was equal to it; and Margaret, the soldier's wife, was equal to it. For her there was her husband's company beside the fire at night; for the long marches of the day, the strangely sweet comradeship of "keep your powder dry!"

And so Zachary and Margaret marched into lone places and made lone bivouacs, while their children learned the ways of the folk back home. But wherever she was, Margaret dreamed of the day when they all would be together in a home that would be their own, a real home, truly theirs. When Zachary was ordered to Baton Rouge after his service in the Seminole War, it seemed as though she were going to realize her dream. As they took up their new station in the South, Margaret spied a little ramshackle cottage that had belonged to the Spanish commandant in the early days of Louisiana; so, instead of moving into the post officers' quarters, she put the old galleried cottage into condition and furnished it for her family.

At last she had a home and even a garden and a grass yard that lazily stretched down to the bank of the Mississippi, where all day long scows, flat boats, meandering rafts, and white and gold river steamers passed on their way up to Natchez or down to New Orleans and the sea.

Margaret had made her last march with Zachary, for when he was given command in the Mexican War he persuaded her to stay on at the "home garrison." While he turned the battles of Palo Alto, Resaca de la Palma, Monterey, and Buena Vista into American victories, she followed his campaign from the news that was brought to her at Baton Rouge. When the post orderly brought her the press dispatches and she read of her husband's steady success in the field, she could not share the surprise of an awed

Betty Taylor, daughter of Zachary Taylor, accepted the duties of hostess in the Executive Mansion from 1849 to 1850.

and admiring American public. From her army years with Zachary she had known that he possessed the powerful will, the tenacity, the driving courage which were directing the American forces against the Mexicans.

But she and Zachary were surprised when that same American public began to talk of making him President of the United States. Neither of them wanted the office for him. Zachary bluntly expressed his ignorance of presidential duties and repeatedly declared that he lacked training for the position. Margaret actually feared that the burden of the position would kill him, and pleaded that he would not accept the nomination. She even prayed that Henry Clay would be nominated—anyone but her husband.

Although Zachary was finally reconciled to the movement to place him in the White House, Margaret never was. She dreaded the enthusiasm with which the public shouted for "Old Rough and Ready, the Hero of Buena Vista."

It was a heavy-hearted, defeated, grieving First Lady who went into the White House that spring of 1849, a First Lady who had reluctantly marched from tent and log cabin and galleried cottage to the most conspicuous "home" in the United States, convinced that her husband was being sacrificed needlessly. For herself, she felt that she was unfitted for the social requirements of her position. Rather than hinder her husband, she shut herself away from public life, surrendering the duties of White House hostess to her daughter Betty.

In the year that she was in the Executive Mansion, she stayed amost entirely in her own suite, leaving it just occasionally to walk in the garden with Zachary. Whenever he could he spent his time with her in the room which she had refurnished to resemble their cottage quarters at Baton Rouge. One very warm July evening in 1850 Zachary, after taking part in a ceremony at the Washington Monument, joined Margaret in that room and confessed to her that he was feeling ill. As she had often done before, in camp and in fort, she nursed him and seldom moved from his side in her battle to win his recovery, but it was the one battle neither of them could win. On July 9 Zachary Taylor died.

Abigail Powers Fillmore
(1798–1853)

INTO a little up-country New York schoolhouse showered a brightness of August sunlight, filled with the dry, sweet smell of mown hay. As its warmth struck against the faces of the "back-bench boys" they stretched out their legs and thought of the cool graveled streams nearby, where trout whipped about in the shadow of the willows.

Even the beginners and intermediates began to scuff their bare feet and to dream lazily of fields and shaded woods; but the thoughts of the tall, wide-eyed girl at the teacher's desk were set on the task before her. Tomorrow was prize day, the end of the summer term, when parents visited school for the closing exercises; there was still much to be done in rehearsing her pupils in their spelling and the Three R's.

She sanded the exercise she had been writing for the intermediates and called the beginners up for spelling. At the sound of her voice the shuffling stopped.

Almost everyone in Sempronius agreed that Abigail Powers was a good teacher. Few schoolmasters managed their classes as smoothly as the auburn-haired girl whose firm, low voice stirred the slowest boy into action; whose friendly manner encouraged the shyest little girl in pinafore to rise from her desk and read; whose steady blue eyes quelled any gesture of defiance from the unruly.

When the schoolhouse was shuttered at the close of prize-day exercises, Abigail wrapped her books and quills, then gave a last look of inspection at the almost deserted room before she started home. As she swung down the road, kicking up little puffs of dust, she sang a chipper old folk air and thought, "I believe I am as glad as the children that school is ended."

It was not because she disliked teaching—she was only twenty-one, but she had been teaching for years. Her father, the Reverend Lemuel Powers, a Baptist country clergyman, had died when she was very young. As soon as she could, Abigail taught school in summer to earn her way through the winter term and to help support her mother. Now that she was teaching both winter and summer school, her vacation was very short; but she especially welcomed it this year, as she could give all of the next few days to working out a study plan for Millard.

She had met him the winter before when they were studying at the same school in Cayuga County, New York. Tall, broad-shouldered Millard Fillmore, the nineteen-year-old wool carder's apprentice, had set his mind on getting an education. Abigail had become interested; so the serious, plodding boy and the serious, quick-minded girl had worked over their problems together. When he took a country school for support, while he studied law, Abigail devoted all her free moments to helping him with his books.

For seven more years she went on teaching in the up-state schoolhouse; then, in 1826, eight years from the time they had first read and studied together, they were married.

So that Millard could devote his time to building up a law practice, Abigail took a school in Aurora. She continued to teach, even after the birth of her first child, until 1830 when they moved to Buffalo and Millard was able to support the family by his own work. In Buffalo Millard entered the political life that was to take him into the White House.

Abigail did not accompany him to Washington for his inauguration as Vice-President of the United States, but she joined him there soon after he took oath of office as President at the death of Zachary Taylor. She found that a greater part of the city had already made itself her friend. Even before she had left Buffalo, residents of Washington were prepared to welcome her, for they knew of the help she had given Millard in his career. She wished that she could do more to repay Washington for its regard; but her health was failing. All that she had strength enough to do was to receive at the weekly Friday-night receptions and preside at the official dinners each Thursday. For other social affairs at the White House her place was taken by her daughter Mary Abigail Fillmore, just graduated from normal school.

Left to herself, Abigail arranged a large second-floor room for her own parlor, and lined it with books bought with an appropriation which Congress granted to President Fillmore for the first library in the White House. As she set the new books in place, she thought of the days when Millard and she had treasured the few, poorly bound books they then owned—an atlas, a geography, a Bible, a psalter, a dictionary. Now she could have *The Great Stone Face* and *The Scarlet Letter* recently written by the brilliant young Hawthorne; *Thanatopsis* by the somber Bryant; the brilliant essays of Emerson; the homely ruddiness of the shy Quaker, Whittier; the neatly turned scholarliness of Lowell, the merry young Harvard graduate. So long as she was in her library, surrounded by her books, Abigail was happy.

She enjoyed, too, evenings when her daughter entertained Millard and her and a few friends, playing on the harp or piano the old songs she loved, or singing the new tunes by Stephen Foster. Then there was the madly gay time when Jenny Lind, the "Swedish Nightingale," sang in Washington. For days the town had talked of nothing but Jenny Lind: how European crowds had drawn her carriage from opera house to hotel. The city was not disappointed.

Like Berlin, Vienna, London, Naples, and New York, it was captured by the blue-eyed "Songbird of the North."

With Lind's concert and the presence in Washington of Henry Clay, General Sam Houston, Daniel Webster, and Stephen A. Douglas, the capital was festive and brilliant even though North and South were quickening their march away from each other. Daily Millard worked for compromise legislation to save the Union. Every evening, after sharp quarrels with Congress, he went to the quiet sitting room where Abigail, his one faithful supporter, awaited him. As in their long-ago school days, he sat by her side and talked of his problems. Together, in Abigail's little sitting room, they strove to save a nation.

Those were the hours she liked best in the White House. She had no desire for the public acclaim given to First Ladies; she was content that the honor of being White House hostess should go to her daughter. All that she wanted was to be a help to Millard, whether he were President of the United States or an unknown lawyer or a wool carder's apprentice trying to get an education. She sought nothing for herself; yet to her, more than to many First Ladies who were brilliant hostesses, went a marked honor, for Abigail Fillmore actually shared the work of a President.

Jane Appleton Pierce
(1806–1863)

THERE was a sudden vicious lurch as the train skittered over a stretch of loose ballast, a grimy cloud of dust and cinders pouring into the coach.

Jane Pierce, grave-eyed and dark, swept the drab film from her lap and smiled ruefully at her husband as she murmured, "And so the Princess rode her milk-white palfrey through lilied meadows to the golden castle upon the hill."

"Traveling nowadays isn't very comfortable or picturesque, is it, Jeanie?" he answered, laughing, settling the shawl round her shoulders again. "And we aren't even going to a castle, just to a boarding house in Washington." They both tightened their faces in a wry expression at the thought of Washington boarding houses, then laughed at each other. "Never mind, Jeanie, we won't be doing this much longer. I won't run for re-election when my term is up next year."

Jane knitted busily for a moment, the bone needles flashing in and out of the half-finished red mittens, then said very earnestly: "Frank, much as I dislike Washington, its crowds and boarding-house life, its scurry of receptions and gossip, I don't want you to give up public life just for me."

For the past few years, ever since her marriage in 1834, she had tried to adapt herself to the active social life demanded of a statesman's wife. She had spent her girlhood in the small Maine town of Brunswick where her father was president of Bowdoin College; her days had been filled with study, her evenings with reading and quiet fireside talk. Her life had been a sheltered one, shut off from crowds and festivity. Now, after eight years of trying to adapt to a new life, she realized that she would always fear it.

She did not want to hear her husband's answer. There was a bleak terror in her heart that he might, just might, ask her to keep on trying; and she was very much afraid that she had not the bravery.

Through the clicking of her needles came the quiet assurance of: "It isn't just because of you, Jeanie. I shall be as glad as you when we get back home to The Elms and my law practice. You know, dear, my office in Concord is really a great deal more comfortable than that cold Senate chamber."

Jane smiled and gratefully tried to believe that Franklin, too, wanted to escape. They were still talking of the pleasant, home hours they would have on their return to The Elms and to their young sons when the conductor came through the car, announcing, "Rainford next. A twenty-minute stop for dinner."

When the whistle screeched for the return to the train, a number were still eating; so they clambered aboard clutching ragged pieces of pie and cake, trailing crumbs along the uncarpeted aisles. A few munched at fruit, dropping the cores and peels alongside their seats.

Soon after the brakeman lighted the candle at each end
of the car, the men hung their hats on wall pegs, propped
their feet high above them on adjoining benches, and prepared to doze through the night. Jane removed her bonnet
and gloves; then, taking a tin basin, towel and a jug of
water from the hamper beside her, went to an end of the
coach. Dabbing at her hands and face, she deftly avoided
the water that every jerk of the train spilled from the basin,
and thought: "Well, anyway, it's better than the way Frank
and I used to travel—perched on the upper deck of a car,
beating out the sparks that the engine threw back on us.
At least we now have a roof over our heads and a stove to
keep us warm in winter."

Returning, she found that Franklin had cushioned the
bare wood bench for her with his coat. She closed her eyes
and tried to sleep. Harried by the jangle and clatter of
the car wheels, she finally gave up all attempt to rest and
spent most of the night watching the passage of the dark
country. Toward morning, she watched eagerly for the
first signs of Washington. As the scarlet and brass engine
pulled its cars into the station, she found the thunderous
ballyhoo of hotel runners almost pleasant, so glad was she
to get out of her train prison.

"This way for the National Hotel!"

"This way for Willard's!"

Shouting runners vied for patronage, snatching baggage
from unwary travelers and quickly stowing it in their carriages, blandly ignoring all protests. Jane and Franklin, sea-
soned in the ways of Washington, kept a firm hold on their
baggage, ignored the bustling runners, and drove to the
boarding house which they had patronized for the past few
years.

At breakfast Jane was greeted by a number of acquaint-
ances, wives of the various Congressmen and Senators, and
clearly heard them explain to those who had not yet met
her: "That's Mrs. Senator Pierce of New Hampshire. She
was Jane Appleton, daughter of the Reverend Jesse Appleton who was president of Bowdoin College, where Senator
Pierce went to school. She is very quiet and does not go
about much, but you will like her. Everyone does."

She was still unpacking trunks and carpetbags when the
door was flung open by a number of Mrs. Secretaries, Mrs.
Senators, and Mrs. Representatives who had come to pay
her an informal call. Jane bowed them to the few chairs,

carefully assigning them places according to the rank of their husbands, then hastily cleared a pile of clothes from the bed to make more sitting room. As they settled themselves, patting their rustling skirts into neat folds and shaking their side curls into place over each ear, Jane closed a trunk and resignedly seated herself on the curved lid. There was little need for her to entertain her guests. As soon as they had advised her of the hairdresser's and a recently opened fruit and vegetable market, they started on their favorite topic, politics.

Jane never took part in the discussions; and seldom did she talk even with Franklin of the current political happenings; but occasionally, when he spoke in the Senate, she took her place in the ladies' gallery to hear him. Bending to bundle her feet in a shawl, she glimpsed Franklin hunching his coat higher on his broad shoulders and jamming his chilled hands into the pockets. Although she was concerned for his comfort she could not help smiling at the boyish impatience with which he summoned a page to put more wood in a glowing iron stove near him.

"I do wish he would consent to wear a shawl here as the rest of the men do," Jane thought, scrutinizing the Senators on the floor, most of whom wore with a grand dignity long dark shawls fastened at the throat with gigantic pins.

"I should think they would even wear their hats, like the Representatives," she told herself. "It certainly would be more sensible than to sit bareheaded all day in this cold draughty place. I do prefer, however, the decorum here; the House is such a bedlam."

As she watched the debating Senators, she recognized several whom she had met, but searched vainly for Henry

Clay's lean figure and friendly smile—Clay, the thin-faced Kentuckian who had enjoyed the reputation of being the most adept snuff-taker in the Senate; then she remembered that the tireless sponsor of compromise legislation had resigned his seat in the Senate the year before. She missed, too, Webster and his brilliance, for he was serving President Tyler as Secretary of State. Jane's thoughts came back to the present when she heard the Vice-President announce, "The Senator from New Hampshire has the floor."

Then Franklin spoke. He gave his carefully pointed speech in the earnest, direct manner which he used in a courtroom. He convinced rather than persuaded or exhorted, and as Jane listened she found herself contrasting the poised speaker to the young lawyer Pierce who had lost his first case. On that humiliating day, he had groped for words; his manner had been awkward; his summing of the case weak. He had failed, but he would not submit to failure, saying: "I will try nine hundred and ninety-nine cases, if the clients will continue to trust me, and, if I fail, as I have today, will try the thousandth. I shall live to argue cases in this courthouse in a manner that will mortify neither myself nor my friends."

He had done more than that. He had advanced to the Senate of the United States; and Jane, unhappy as she was in Washington, was proud of that advance.

He did not, however, finish his term in the Senate, but surprised his colleagues by resigning in 1842. Nor would he leave The Elms again when President Polk invited him to join his cabinet as Attorney General. He declined the honor, writing: "When I resigned my seat in the Senate in 1842, I did it with the fixed purpose never again to be voluntarily separated from my family for any considerable length of time, except at call of my country in time of war."

That call came soon, when annexation of Texas brought on war with Mexico. At the first call for troops Franklin enlisted as a private, but was soon commissioned a brigadier general by President Polk. His bravery in the Puebla campaign became famous when, so severely hurt that he had to be lifted into his saddle, he insisted upon leading his men into battle.

On his return to Concord he again took up his law practice and, in 1848, refused the nomination for the office of state governor. He was keeping faith with Jane in his determination to stay out of public office. Four years later he was still firm in that decision; but, despite his opposition, he was named Democratic candidate for the presidency of the United States and, almost against his will, was voted into office. At forty-nine he was the youngest man to have been elected President.

Jane prepared to move into the White House, somewhat comforted in the belief that she would have her only son, Benjamin, there with her. Since the death of Franklin junior in 1843 her life had centered in Benjamin, and he accompanied her everywhere. Just a few weeks before the inauguration of Franklin, Jane and he took the boy with them on a short railroad trip out of Concord. There was a wreck, and the boy was killed.

Jane never fully recovered from the shock of the tragedy; yet, as soon as she could, she summoned back enough strength to join Franklin in Washington. She was First Lady of the Land, but there had never been so sad a First Lady as Jane Pierce. And yet Washington—the city enriched by the gaiety of Dolley Madison, the pioneer pluck of Abigail Adams, the regality of Elizabeth Monroe—took few First Ladies so into its heart as it did the gentle, grieving wife of Franklin Pierce.

At the public receptions she was at Franklin's side, standing for hours to give her hand to all the guests; at the formal dinners and public ceremonies she was in the honored place appointed to her. All of her life she had retreated from public contact, so sensitive to its demands that she was afraid of it. When she finally faced the test, there in the White House, she made herself equal to it even to her last day as First Lady when, her strength nearly exhausted, she was carried from the Executive Mansion.

Harriet Lane Johnston
(1833–1903)

SCRAMBLING and burrowing, Harriet dug into the woodpile and hurled chunk after chunk of kindling into the stave barrow at her side. Then, seizing the handles, she squared her heels into the ground and lunged forward from the shoulders, pushing mightily to move the load toward the path.

A raw wind stung her hands, and her breath made a mist in the air; but her face grew hot with exertion, and the light hair at her forehead curled into damp ringlets beneath her bonnet. The cumbersome wheelbarrow gained momentum on a slope, and when James Buchanan chanced to look from his study window he saw a wavering, plunging load of wood, a whirling torrent of legs, skirts, and a bonnet that now trailed rakishly behind Harriet on its strings.

"Harriet! Har-ri-et!" The voice of James Buchanan, United States Senator from Pennsylvania, was resonant and, when he shouted as he did then, very commanding. "Har-ri-et!"

Legs, skirts, bonnet, and wheelbarrow somehow came to a stop. "Yes, Uncle James."

Summoning a senatorial dignity, Buchanan addressed the

tousled child below the window: "May I ask what madcap idea promoted this latest burst of unseemly conduct from you? Why should you, a young lady eleven years old, your clothes awry, race down the lane, propelling a wheelbarrow full of wood?"

With a direct honesty, Harriet answered merely, "Aunt Tabitha was cold; so I was taking her some kindling for a fire, Uncle James."

Buchanan, glad that his niece had thought of the old lady who was cared for by the neighborhood, rebuked her "unseemly conduct" very gently and sent the wood and some food to Aunt Tabitha's cottage. Harriet went into the house to practice sewing.

At fifty-three, James Buchanan had fixed ideas regarding etiquette, and for two years he had been trying to rear Harriet according to them. It had been a two years of surprises for him, surprises which began on the very day that the orphaned Harriet had looked about at the relatives gathered round her and selected him, her bachelor uncle, to be her guardian.

His delight, however, equaled the surprise, and he immediately took her home with him to Wheatland, his small estate near Lancaster, where Harriet lost no time in taking command of the household. There was the time when Buchanan found her sliding down the hall near his study, zealously trying for a new distance record at each swoop, and suggested that she play in the garden. Scarcely was he settled in his chair to talk with visiting political colleagues when up through the window came the writhing howl of an Indian war cry, proudly hurled from the robust throat of niece Harriet. Buchanan's amused colleagues heard him sigh as he strode to the window and ordered her to return

to the house and be quiet. What they did not understand
was why he smiled widely a few minutes later, then waved
his hands as though to motion someone away from the
door: they could not see Harriet who stood behind them,
impishly caricaturing them with gestures and grimaces.

After trying for two years to cope with her escapades,
Buchanan found that she had almost a genius for tearing
clothes, bumping and scratching her hands and face, throw-
ing a civilized household into uproar, and making herself
dear to him in spite of it all. She tried his patience, strained
his sense of humor, and he was very glad that she had chosen
him to be her guardian. Years later, when she was a grown
woman, a friend questioned him about Harriet's turbulent
childhood, and Buchanan answered: "She never told a lie.
She had a soul above deceit or fraud. She was too proud
for it."

He found it hard to decide that she must go away to
school, but because he felt that the training was imperative,
he finally called Harriet into his study and told her that
she was to leave Wheatland. Watching her, he could not
determine who was the unhappier, he or the child who was
trying hard not to cry, scuffing her dusty shoes miserably
against each other, twisting her fingers in a rumpled apron.
When she went, first to Charleston, then to the convent at
Georgetown, her thoughts were devoted to the vacation
weeks when she would be with Uncle James again.

The Harriet who graduated from the Georgetown convent was very different from the Harriet who had whirled
down the Wheatland path after a wheelbarrow. She was
still straight, her blond head erect, her eyes a clear violet;
but she was lithe, her movements assured and graceful, her
voice and laugh quieted. As she accompanied Buchanan,

then Ambassador to England, to the royal court, even Queen Victoria noted her beauty. Victoria was thoroughly charmed by the young American, and favored her with the rank of an ambassador's wife, so according her a court precedence which she would not have commanded as merely the niece of an ambassador.

But it was in her own country that Harriet enjoyed the great honor of her life, that of presiding at the White House. Not since Dolley Madison had there been a First Lady who so plunged into the complicated regime at the Executive Mansion. Harriet, at twenty-four, began her leadership the very night of Buchanan's inauguration, accompanying him to the ball given by the city.

Washington in 1857 was almost riotously happy, even though threats of a shattered Union were increasing daily. The North had so long heard the Southern challenge that it was beginning to shrug, negligently, at the warning. Washington, particularly, seemed content to live in the moment; so President Buchanan's inaugural ball was a very grand party at which laughing, dancing Washington did its best to make way with one hundred twenty-five gallons of chicken salad, four hundred gallons of oysters, muttons, hams, beef, tongues, venison, five hundred quarts of jellies, and three hundred gallons of ice cream. It was a very grand party, and Washington accepted it as the herald of a revived gaiety in the White House.

Nor was the city disappointed in the new First Lady who filled the White House with flowers and livened the receptions and "at homes" by a captivating mixture of spontaneity and regal beauty. Even when just her own friends surrounded her at a piano in one of the smaller parlors, their songs and teasing laughter swept the White House with an animation that it had long lacked. Outside there might be a gloom of rain; in the Capitol buildings on the hill there might be a brittle grimness of accusation and defiance— abolitionist and slaveholder; but in the White House there were youth and gay banter. The young people talked little of the Dred Scott decision but much of their own billowing crinolines and flowered cravats; little of "Bleeding Kansas," much of the new song, "The Mocking Bird," which had been dedicated to Harriet, and of the novel *Rutledge* which an admiring public had attributed mistakenly to her pen.

They were interested, too, in the news from France, not through a taste for European politics, but because the life or death of the crinoline depended on the Parisian style dictum. So far the American fashionables were in vogue with their enormous skirts, for the Empress Eugénie was still champion of the crinoline. When the transatlantic post brought word that the fanciful, romantic wife of Napoleon III had appeared at a court ball in a straight and flowing gown, Washington girls put away their cages their whalebone skirts and treasured crinolines. Their escorts were jubilant—they had had their own difficulties in trying to dance with partners in crinolines, in driving them about in smart but cramped gigs and cutters.

It was a White House of heedless happy youth; a Washington that daily talked of crises and seemed not to realize of what it talked; a country that listened, and waited helplessly. In the President's chair there was a bewildered man, too little of a leader to win the nation's faith. Dazed by the growing turmoil, he was glad to lose himself now and then in the gala triviality of social display. Together, Harriet and he gave a brilliance to hospitality in the Executive Mansion, climaxing the festivity with an entertainment for the visiting Prince of Wales. Because there were no guest facilities in the White House, Buchanan gave his room to the young prince and slept on a couch in his office.

It all ended, this social extravaganza, when John Brown made his raid into Virginia on October 16, 1860. Washington no longer talked of crises—the crisis was at hand. The stunned man in the President's chair still delayed action; but the nation expected all that followed, expected that South Carolina would secede when Abraham Lincoln was elected President, that the other Southern states would also withdraw from the Union. In the hotels and Congressional boarding houses a number of women already flaunted secession cockades; but in the Executive Mansion there were two tragical figures, one broken by his inability to help his country, the other because she knew not how to help him. The two who had brought to the White House a splendor of accomplishment and youth carried from it, on March 4, 1861, the heartbreak of failure.

Mary Todd Lincoln
(1818–1882)

HER face flushed, she stood at the door of the Blue Room. Her breath caught in her throat as she suddenly reached out her hands, whispering, "It's mine, my very own! At last it's mine!"

In the moment that she darted about the parlor, picking at draperies and curtains, she pictured the teas and thronged receptions she would have in this very room—with herself, Mary Todd Lincoln, presiding as mistress of the White House, as First Lady of the Land. But even as she seated herself, impetuously fancying that scores of fashionably dressed guests encircled her chair, her hands found a sticky mass on the upholstered edge and she withdrew her fingers to find them stained. Instantly she was on her feet, examining all of the furniture.

From the doorway came a familiar voice, high and bantering, "Well, Mother, have you found something wrong already? Even in the White House of your dreams?"

Before Lincoln reached her with his great flat stride, Mary whirled upon him to cry, "Abra'am, we shall have to clean this whole house, and I don't see how we can afford to do it. Every politician in the country must have set his

muddy boots on the furniture. And this is the very room where I had wanted to hold my levees. We'll have to sell everything we can, Abra'am, to get the money to clean up this place."

Her last words were muffled against Lincoln's breast as he gathered her into his long arms. "It's going to be all right now, Mother. We were always poor in Springfield, but you gave some of the largest and nicest parties in town, and when I didn't have any money you somehow kept the stew-pot boiling for us. Now that we are here where you always wanted us to be, we shall manage somehow; so you just go ahead and get the house fixed up the way you like it, and I won't forget to take you to cotillions, the way I used to do sometimes back in our courting days."

Tears still in her eyes, Mary smiled and caught Lincoln's hand to her side, answering with some of her girlhood coquetry, "And maybe I shall waltz again with Douglas—the way *I* used to do sometimes back in our courting days. But, then, I chose the right man, didn't I, Abra'am, to bring me into the White House?"

She smoothed his glistening white shirt that the pressure of her head had ruffled, then chanced to look up into his face, seeing as always only the gravely tender gray eyes. She added very softly, "I chose the right man, anyway, Abra'am."

When he left her for his office Mary went through the White House, from top to bottom, finding her thoughts a strange mixture of domestic detail and comparisons of her old with her new life. Now, as mistress of the Executive Mansion, she, the descendant of General Andrew Porter and the Todds of Virginia, was in a social order for which her birth and training had prepared her. Now Abra'am was in his proper place as a leader of men. Once, such a short time ago, she had been confined to a little downstate Illinois town, trying to make both ends meet on the tiny and spasmodic earnings of an Abra'am who was moody with defeat, boisterous with uncertain humor, careless and shabby—but the man she had chosen, the man whose genius looked out from somber gray eyes.

Their journey to Washington had been strange. From the moment they had entered the train at Springfield, chilled by a drift of rain, conductors had searched the seats for bombs; after every stop trainmen, grim in their fear of attempted assassination, examined every inch of the presidential car while brakemen tapped at the wheels to insure no breakage. New York greeted Lincoln and his party with a great parade. Crowds closed in after his carriage to follow it to the hotel, some loud in their surprise that Abra'am was not so ugly nor so ungainly as rumor and cartoons had made him. Mary had been proud of him. When he appeared on the hotel gallery to address the crowd, he was as neatly groomed and self-possessed as Hamlin, the Vice-President-elect who stood beside him. His voice deepened as his speech progressed, and she could see the listening people respond to his understanding smile and hear them cheer "Honest Abe, the coming man."

But in Baltimore the journey ended in the threatening shadows in which it had begun, for in Baltimore there was an uneasiness which forced Abra'am to leave Mary and proceed without her to Washington in the shelter of night.

He had been saved from any danger in Baltimore, which seethed with secession talk, and no harm befell him at his inauguration, when troops lined the street and marksmen lay on roofs guarding the presidential stand.

Abra'am and she had reached the White House to face a new sort of life. Much as she had dreamed of it, as she had longed for it, she fully realized the difference between the old and new life only when she made her entry at the inaugural ball. When she heard the band swing into "Hail to the Chief" and saw the broad stooped figure of Lincoln confidently striding ahead of her, she felt for the first time that it was really Abra'am and she.

Then someone bowed over her hand, but it was not Abra'am who was asking her for a quadrille. It was Stephen Douglas, wise from many political victories and gallant from his years in the Senate; but his eyes were still challenging in their bold blue, his jaw still aggressive in its jutting thrust; and he was the same, though much older, Douglas who had squired Mary in Springfield. Smiling as she thought of the political rivalry which had so long existed between her husband and the "Little Giant," Mary accepted Douglas' invitation and took his arm to dance. Almost everyone turned to see how Mrs. Lincoln would deport herself. Some had been amused at the very thought of a prairie lawyer's plump wife having the place of honor in Washington; yet as they watched, they saw Mary as a composed, a not ungraceful woman in blue silk, in her hair a blue ostrich plume. They looked, and they gossiped about her, then went to eat the $4,000 inaugural-ball supper.

They gossiped about her at her own receptions, at her own dinner table, while she wondered if she could be as hateful as they said. One supporter came to her, however. He was the elegant Charles Sumner, Senator from Massachusetts and a Harvard graduate. As they talked with Lincoln in Mary's parlor, Sumner was quick to discover her keen knowledge of politics, her impulsive but generally correct judgment of people, her interest in literature. In their talk of poetry one day he thoughtlessly veered into a phrase of French, instantly flushing in the belief that he had embarrassed his hostess with a superior gesture; but before he could make polite amends, Mary completed the quotation.

"Your accent is far more Parisian than any American's that I've heard, Mrs. Lincoln," commented Sumner, not quite able to control the surprise in his voice. "But I thought you had never been abroad."

Lincoln was enjoying the elegant Sumner's confusion when Mary answered, "Nor have I, Senator. That little patch of French goes back to my Kentucky days. I was educated at Madame Mentelle's private school in Lexington, where we spoke only in that tongue all day long. Once my French was so fluent that I raged at the preceptress for minutes on end without calling on English, but it has slipped from me after years of disuse."

Sumner's smile at the idea of a little Southern miss in pantalets and hoop skirts having a tantrum in French was brief. He suddenly realized the tragedy of that temper—seeing, as though he had been watching her all through the harried years, the dashing little Southerner grow into a woman driven by an overpowering will.

But not even Sumner knew of the rash extravagance with which Mary was assembling a wardrobe. All of her life she had loved display. As the daughter of a Lexington banker she had been fashionably dressed, but then had come the drawn years as wife of Abraham Lincoln whose disregard of money had so often enraged her. Now that she held the most prominent social position in the nation, she tried to make up for all that had been denied her. Thinking only of the moment, she plunged into an irresponsible shopping spree, buying dresses, cloaks, shawls, bonnets, and jewelry.

As she stood in her room dressing for a levee, she was not thinking of tradesmen and shopkeepers who had turned her head with flattery and given her unlimited credit. She was deciding what jewels to wear that evening.

She heard a laugh from the garden and, without looking, she knew that Abra'am was out there playing with Willie and Tad, his stiff dark hair rumpled as he threw back his head to laugh. As she walked to the window her memory caught at other pictures of Abra'am—the Abra'am who used to stride down Springfield streets pulling a shambling wagon full of children, his head drooped in thought as he pondered in his slow way; dropping his weathered green cotton umbrella and tilting back his hat, while the letters and papers under his arm threatened to fall to the ground, as he knuckled down to a game of marbles with Willie's friends.

There in the garden was the same Abra'am who used to take off his coat, shoes, and dingy stock to lie on the parlor floor while he read aloud from books of poetry or newspapers; the Abra'am who would sit at the dinner table staring silently at his plate, ignoring food, then without warning burst into laughter, snap again into secretive gloom, and finally tear through his meal as though he did not know or care what he was eating; the moody Abra'am she had married in 1842, almost two years after he had failed to appear on the day originally set for the ceremony.

Even now, in the White House garden, his tie was askew, and the tails of his neat broadcloth coat flapped riotously as he wrestled with Willie and Tad. He had been summoned to the Cabinet Room at five o'clock that morning, and had spent all day in his office, begrudging even the few minutes that Mary forced him to give to luncheon. In the tussle with his sons he was having his only relaxation, and Mary felt that his loud laugh and tousled hair were good. Before she called to remind him of dressing for the levee, she decided that she would make him ride every afternoon with her in their carriage. He must, she fiercely encouraged herself, get away from his office sometime during the day.

They went down to the levee together—Abra'am brushed and polished, the stoop of his shoulders adding a peculiar dignity to his long spare figure; Mary, scented and powdered, in crimson silk, her throat and shoulders bare, her head encircled by a wreath of flowers.

At the entrance to the Blue Room, Mary stiffened. Her fingers bit into Abra'am's arm. Quickly he looked from the almost empty room into Mary's eyes and saw there not familiar glints of anger, but a look of desolation. He was not prepared for the tragedy he heard in Mary's voice. "Abra'am, they aren't coming to see me. They don't want me here in the White House."

"Now, Mother, we have a hard place to fill here," he began as he turned her aside until she could find control of herself.

Mary seemed not to have heard him, for she went on in a deadened voice, "They think I am a Rebel sympathizer, Abra'am, because I come from Kentucky. They say I pass information to the Confederate armies. They say I'm not loyal to you and the Union, Abra'am. They say . . . oh, Abra'am!"

Lincoln picked up the fan she had dropped and, catching both her hands in one of his, closed them firmly about it. "Come, Mother, our guests are waiting. They aren't many, but they are our guests, and you must not forget your duties as hostess in the President's house. Come, now, I see Sumner out there, and there's Douglas, too. Ready?"

Mary's head went up and she bit her lips to bring back their color. "Yes, Abra'am. I am ready." And she walked unseeing into the room which was to have housed the brilliant reception of her dreams, into the room which now sheltered so few guests.

While Washington talked of her as a Confederate sympathizer, Mary smiled bitterly and spent much of her time visiting Union hospitals in the city, helping staffs with organization details, and cheering wounded veterans. When Stoddard, a secretary to Lincoln, suggested that she quiet the gossip about her disloyalty by allowing the city to know of her hospital work, she refused. She would not publicly demand sympathy.

At last it seemed to her as though everything were going to come out all right. After four years Lee had surrendered to Grant. Lincoln had been re-elected, and Tad was daily taking more of her thoughts from Willie, the son who had died in the White House. The nation hailed Grant as the hero of Appomattox, Lee as the chivalrous leader of a lost cause, and Lincoln as the savior of the Union. In her joy Mary persuaded Abra'am to accompany her to the theater— her favorite sort of entertainment—just to celebrate the end of the old years of trial and the beginning of the new years of honor and contentment.

They went to Ford's Theater on Good Friday evening, April 14, 1865; and John Wilkes Booth withheld the new years of honor and contentment from Abra'am and Mary, for he killed those years when he killed Abra'am.

Not for five weeks was Mary, shattered in health, able to leave the White House; then, in a frantic realization of the debts she had to meet, she stripped the mansion of all her personal things, of all the gifts that had been presented to the family, and shipped them to Chicago until time to convert them into money for payment of her enormous bills. Almost before her train pulled out for Chicago she heard that Washington was saying that she had stolen furniture and silver from the White House.

For the next seventeen years, until her death at the Springfield home of her sister, Mrs. Ninian W. Edwards, Mary knew little but sorrow. There were trips to Europe in search of health; the death of Tad; Sumner's hard-won victory for her pension; the injury to her spine when she fell in her little Paris apartment; the last helpless days in the house where Abra'am had courted her; death in the room near that in which he had married her.

Eliza McCardle Johnson
(1810–1876)

INDIAN summer, a drowsy warmth filled with smoke of burning leaves, settled down on the Tennessee mountain village of Greeneville, and Main Street seemed to sleep in the sunlight that autumn afternoon of 1826 when Eliza McCardle chose her future husband.

She had been admiring a pink parasol in the window of the general store but, at a burst of laughter from her companions, quickly turned to see what was amusing them. She saw what they saw, but she didn't laugh.

Coming down Main Street was a strange jumble of groaning wagon, plodding horse, chairs and tables, pots and pans. She could have smiled at the gangling array of furniture on the ramshackle wagon, but in the tired face of the wide-shouldered, black-haired boy who was leading the cavalcade there was a determination and a strength that impressed her.

She was still watching him as one of her friends laughed. "What a handsome beau he will make for some Greeneville girl—when he gets his face washed!"

"Don't laugh, Sarah," Eliza insisted. "I like him."

Others grew to like him; he opened a tiny shop, hung out

a sign, "A. Johnson, Tailor," and went to work with needle and shears to support his mother. His face was washed, his clothes clean and neat, but he had not forgotten the poverty of his childhood and apprentice days in Raleigh, North Carolina, when his mother fed and clothed him on her scant earnings as a weaver. As he cut and sewed in his little two-room shop, she was his first consideration. Next in his mind was thought of Eliza McCardle, seventeen and brown-haired, daughter of a Scotch shoemaker, who had not laughed at him when he first walked into Greeneville from Raleigh.

Nor did anyone laugh when Eliza and he were married in May of 1827. The industrious young tailor of the rugged face and sharp dark eyes already commanded respect; and the attitude with which his eighteen-year-old bride set about making a home for him in the back room of the shop showed a courage which Greeneville found admirable. Eliza more than made a home for him. She prepared him for the career that was to take him to the presidency of the United States.

In his apprentice days at Raleigh, Andrew had taught himself to spell and read. In the tailor shop at Greeneville, Eliza taught him arithmetic and how to write. As he sat cross-legged on his bench, she read aloud to him while he cut and stitched. At night after dinner, they again went into the shop where Eliza set paper and pens before him and guided his hand in letter making. She felt a tightness in her throat as she watched his first efforts—the letters were so pinched, so uncertain, like a child's. But as he practiced night after night—his broad shoulders stooped over the table, his strong, heavy hand tight around a quill pen—the writing became bolder and manlike. The teacher was proud of her pupil, and the pupil was just as proud of his teacher.

Eliza quickly found that politics captured his interest; so she helped him collect a store of clippings from newspapers and magazines, and they read as many speeches as they could find. While he practiced stump speaking she acted as audience, aiding him with her suggestions to build logic and conviction into his political talks.

Their daughter Martha was born the year he was elected to his first public office, that of a Greeneville alderman, but Eliza still found time to study with him. As he advanced into state and national politics she took up a new work. The pupil no longer needed a teacher, but he did need someone to care for his private business while he devoted himself to public office; so Eliza became the business manager of the household. While he served in the state legislature and in Congress, she stayed at Greeneville, schooling her family, collecting rents, and directing improvements on the land and buildings which they had thriftily bought.

She was there in the little mountain town when President Lincoln appointed Andrew, then United States Senator, to be Military Governor of Tennessee. While he established himself at Nashville and directed defense of the capitol against Confederate armies, Eliza remained in Greeneville, refusing to desert her home and property even though she was surrounded by hostile secessionists. Her efforts were futile, for the Confederates confiscated the property and converted her home into a barracks and hospital for their own troops while they ordered Eliza to leave Greeneville and pass through the Southern lines.

Her husband's name was hated throughout the Confederate South because he supported Lincoln and the Union; so there were few who dared to help her on the way to

Nashville and to Andrew. But, though she was ill and very nearly exhausted by the journey, it was no cringing "traitor" who made her way into Nashville and the barricaded capitol that October day of 1862. In her feebly erect walk and in her tired eyes was the same courage which had sent her as a bride into the drab little tailor shop on Main Street, the same pride in her husband with which she had prepared him for a career.

She was just as proud of him in his stubborn defense of the capitol as she was three years later when he took office as Vice-President of the United States—proud but not surprised, for the boy whom she had so patiently taught had grown into a man whose honesty and dauntless sense of duty impressed an entire nation.

With him she went into the White House, when he succeeded to the presidency at the death of Abraham Lincoln, but her days of active help were ended by illness which confined her to her room. The teacher had done all that she could, and it was for the pupil to work with what she had taught him and what he had so well learned. All that she could give him in the White House was her steadying companionship when his temper threatened to overpower his judgment, comfort when he tired of fighting a hostile Congress that destroyed his effort to spread peace and friendship through the defeated South. She alone was able to quiet his anger when he saw the Congressional Radicals ignore the conciliating program of reconstruction that had been Lincoln's ideal and which Andrew tried to carry out for his dead chief, when they overrode his vetoes and put the helpless South under military rule. To the quiet upper room in the White House he would storm, distracted by the injustice he was powerless to prevent, and it was only when he could take Eliza's hand and find comfort in her gentle understanding that he felt he could again take up his fight. Eliza, who would have given anything to be able to leave her invalid's chair and be with him more, was happiest when she knew that her daughter Martha was at his side.

It was Martha, the wife of Senator David Patterson of Tennessee, who acted as First Lady for her father. It was Martha who, when she first went into the White House, had made scores of friends in Washington by saying to a newspaper reporter: "We are a plain people, sir, from the mountains of Tennessee, and we do not propose to put on airs because we have the fortune to occupy this place for a little while."

As soon as she had arranged for her invalid mother's comfort, Martha made a thorough inspection of the White House, and found it a shambles. Thousands of people had entered the mansion during the war days, seeking pardons and favors from President Lincoln; sentries had paced the halls and guarded the stairs; orderlies had delivered dispatches day and night; throngs had swept through the rooms to view the catafalque on which the assassinated Lincoln lay.

Martha found the carpets torn by sabers and spurs; heavy boots had ground mud into them and into the furniture where tired soldiers had stretched out to rest while waiting for President Lincoln. Broken chairs and torn curtains evidenced the turmoil that had raged in the wartime White House.

Martha was First Lady, but she organized the servants into a scrubbing and scouring corps. For several days she changed into a house dress immediately after breakfast to lead her company of cleaners on a campaign of reclaiming the White House from the neglect into which it had fallen during Mrs. Lincoln's illness. Until luncheon they flooded the floors with great waves of soapy water and vigorously scrubbed into every corner; then Martha dressed for the afternoon to receive callers at the Mansion, and none suspected that a few hours earlier she had been in the midst of drastic house cleaning.

When Washington learned that the First Lady had bought two Jersey cows and milked them every morning to supply fresh cream for the White House table no one thought to gossip scornfully of her. In this "plain woman from the mountains of Tennessee," Washington found an integrity which Greeneville had found in her father and mother, the young tailor and his bride of eighteen who had made their own way and asked help from no one.

Martha might milk cows every morning and set her clean milk pails in the greenhouse; but Washington was very glad to attend her teas and her receptions in the evening. Everyone was always sure of a welcome, even though Congress had lashed Johnson with talk of impeachment. Throughout those harried months of the impeachment fight, Martha seldom left her father's side during the hours he was away from his desk. Martha was glad they were alone when word came that one vote had saved him from impeachment, for she was not sure she would have been able to face the public with her usual composure. Her father had suffered too much. In his surrender to happiness at news of acquittal she saw for the first time the strain under which he had been carrying the presidential duties. She wondered if she could ever again amicably face those who had attacked his honor, cruelly burdening him with disgrace.

Yet for his last levee, when more than five thousand people sought admittance to the White House, she was again at his side to make her farewells as graciously as though she did not know there had been an impeachment trial. It was hard, but she had her mother's pride and her father's courage; so Martha Johnson Patterson went out from the White House in 1869 with the regard and admiration of a city that was critical of First Ladies.

Not even Martha, however, knew how her mother suffered throughout the impeachment trial. No longer able to be at his side, Eliza could only sit helpless in her room as she waited for news of the struggle to dishonor her husband.

Her joy at news of the acquittal was great, but full happiness came to her a few years later when Andrew 'was returned to the Senate, and she knew then that his country
had restored him to its service in a place of honor. Once
more the nation gave tribute to him, and that tribute meant
more to Eliza than the oath which had placed him in the
President's chair. She was not First Lady, but when Andrew
took his seat in the Senate she was the proudest, happiest
lady in the land.

Julia Dent Grant

(1826–1902)

"How do I look, Dent?" asked the slender man with the boyish face and sleepy eyes.

"Well, Ulyss, to tell the truth, I have seen you in clothes that fitted you better, that didn't hide you from sight, as it were. But if you will put your horse across the creek in flood water, you ought to consider yourself lucky to find a dry suit waiting, even if it is big enough for two of you. Hey! Wait a minute. You forgot to put on a stock."

Dent flung out of the room after him, the black satin tie dangling from his hand, but there was a grim haste in the stride of the fleeing Ulysses S. Grant that deterred his host from following him. As Dent watched the slim figure, in its flapping suit of borrowed clothes, march down the hall, he wondered, "What's up? Never saw Ulyss stir himself into such action before. Must have something important on his mind."

Grant did have something important on his mind. Ordinarily even his drenched clothes would not have turned him from a direct course to his goal. But when he had reached White Haven, a few minutes earlier, and looked down at his bedraggled regimentals, he had decided that he made a sorry figure for the exciting project before him.

Now that he was there and changed into dry things, what should he say? What should he do? Well, it was a principle of his never to turn back until he had reached his goal, and he was not going to fail now.

"Ulyss, whatever makes you storm along like a thundercloud! Aren't you going to visit with me a minute?" Julia Dent noted her brother's suit on Grant, and her eyes twinkled at the unhappy fit of the clothes, but her slow voice and easy manner confessed to no amusement.

Grant had almost passed her by in his struggle of perplexed thoughts. At the sound of the familiar drawl he snapped around on his heel to take up the business that had brought him through a flooded creek to White Haven.

"Julia, I have been ordered with the regiment to the frontier at Louisiana," he began, much as though he were making a report at General Headquarters. "We join General Taylor's Army of Observation in case of trouble with Mexico over Texas. Julia, I love you."

Then Lieutenant Ulysses S. Grant of the Fourth United States Infantry, more accustomed to giving orders than to making pleas, made a plea that won him the hand of eighteen-year-old Julia Dent.

That was in May of 1844. They planned to be married just as soon as Grant was released from service in the Mexican War, and that would not be long to wait, they thought. But he was in the field four years. While he was fighting at Monterey, Vera Cruz, and San Cosme with the valor that won him a brevet captaincy, Julia waited at White Haven, her father's plantation near St. Louis. Captain Grant came for her there in the summer of 1848, and they were married on August 22—at first to be very happy, then to struggle for a living, to be engulfed by fame, to struggle again, and to win.

For a few years their life was similar to that of all young army couples stationed at frontier posts; uneventful years at garrisons in Sackett's Harbor, New York, and in Detroit; two years of separation while Grant served on the Pacific coast and Julia lived again at White Haven, because Grant would not allow her to make the rigorous trip to California.

When, in the summer of 1854, he again went to get Julia at the plantation, he had resigned his commission in the army.

"What do you want to do, Ulyss?" asked Julia.

"I thought I would try farming." Then, with his slow quizzical smile, "But I guess we shall have to call our farm 'Hardscrabble' for a while, Julia, because we shan't be able to start out with a big place like this."

"That's all right. I have land of my own near St. Louis and we shall make our start there," was her confident answer.

So they took their growing family from White Haven, and went to make their second start at Hardscrabble, where Grant built the house with his own hands and put his own shoulders to the plow while Julia cooked and sewed and cleaned as cheerfully as though she were still mistress of a great plantation house. For four years they tried to make a living from the farm, while Grant even cut and carted firewood for sale in St. Louis; then in the fall of 1858, after illness had disabled him, Julia and he watched the auctioneer sell all their farm goods and stock.

In the two years that followed, Julia would not admit defeat, but Grant realized that he was beaten, that his business attempts in St. Louis were leading to nothing. There seemed but one thing to do. They moved to Galena, Illinois, where he became a clerk in his father's leather-goods store.

Throughout that winter in Galena there was little promise that their life would again change. As a clerk's wife, Julia was as serene and interested in her daily affairs as she had been on the plantation where slaves had always been at hand to wait upon her. In the store, Grant was a quiet and unusually accommodating clerk who weighed and sold leather, saying no unnecessary words, but talking in a friendly and almost gentle manner when he did speak. Customers liked to have him wait upon them. At home he lost his taciturnity to joke and tussle with his sons, until Julia could see in him again the carefree, sleepy-eyed young lieutenant who had escorted her to dances at Jefferson Barracks and St. Louis plantations.

On April 11, 1861, South Carolina fired upon Fort Sumter in Charleston harbor. The shots sounded the opening of the Civil War; they saluted the beginning of new days for Grant and his wife.

The clerk marched into the field as colonel of the Twenty-first Illinois Volunteers, and within a few weeks the straps of a brigadier general were placed on his shoulders. Ulysses S. Grant was no longer the beaten man who had walked the streets of St. Louis looking for work to support his family. As General Grant he became the alert soldier, the fearless, canny soldier of whom President Lincoln was to say: "I can't spare him. He's a fighter."

With Grant returned to the service, Julia again became an "army woman," eager to share campaign life as much as possible with her husband. Few were steadier under fire than she. She was at Holly Springs, Mississippi, a secondary base of supplies for Grant's forces, when the Confederates

captured the garrison. Warned by a staff officer that she, the wife of General Grant, must not be captured, Julia tucked her four-year-old son Jesse under her arm and quickly threaded her way through the confusion to the railroad, where she clambered into a box car just before the train pulled out to safety.

She had no thought of danger when she carried Jesse up the gangplank for the trip down the Mississippi to join Grant at Vicksburg. Two great paddle wheels took hold, and sent the steamer into the channel. Even after they had gone to their cabin they could feel the deck quiver and lurch under the rumbling drive of the paddles. But the noise that wakened Julia, a few hours later, was the brisk hard noise of shots. Confederate sympathizers were shelling the steamer from hidden guns on the shore.

Again and again throughout the war Julia heard the dull thud of bullets beating into wood, the shrill scream of bullets winging overhead; heard the sharp call of bugles, the challenge of sentries, the ominously patient pounding of siege guns. Pounding, pounding—steadily, doggedly, like "Unconditional Surrender" Grant himself—until gray-clad Confederates returned home to build a new South from the old, and Union troops made their final march under arms, swinging up Pennsylvania Avenue in Washington to salute the man who had led them to victory.

"Grant! Grant! Goodbye, old man!" called that long blue line of the Army of the Potomac and the Army of the West, as it followed Meade and Sherman past the reviewing stand where Grant watched his soldiers march by for the last time, their torn battle flags waving high above their bayonets.

They said goodbye and gave him a last salute as their wartime chief; but those veterans of Shiloh and the Wilder-

The President and Mrs. Grant arriving at the Inaugural Ball

ness did not forget him—three years after Appomattox they chose him to be their peacetime chief, and he was inaugurated President of the United States on March 4, 1869.

Just eleven years after Julia and he had left Hardscrabble they moved into the White House, and neither of them was very much changed.

Throughout her eight years as First Lady, Julia gave the greater part of her time to welcoming the public to the White House, being as cordial to visiting delegations of Union veterans as though she had not been summoned from the luncheon table just a moment before. Little as she cared for social activity, she responded so gracefully to her duties as hostess that at the end of Grant's second term as President she had won a popularity which rivaled his.

At their return to private life in 1877 they took a long holiday, making a trip around the world, so confident were they that the Hardscrabble days were over forever. When they returned to New York, Grant went into business. He had been in business before and had failed, and now he was again defeated. Julia and he lost all that they had.

But Grant refused to stay defeated. He had, somehow, to provide for Julia. His health was broken, but he fought to keep alive until he could write his memoirs, so that there would be royalties to support Julia after his death.

With her at his side he wrote his personal history of the Civil War until he could no longer move a pencil, then he whispered dictation of the last chapters. In this last fight he showed his unbreakable will as he made a forced march to his last victory, struggling day after day to win protection for the woman who had never lost faith in him during his early days of defeat. It was for her that he strove after and won that last victory.

Lucy Webb Hayes
(1831–1889)

O<small>N</small> December 30, 1852, Lucy slipped into her bridal dress for the first time and walked down to the parlor of her mother's Cincinnati home for her marriage to young Rutherford Birchard Hayes. On December 30, 1877, she again put on her wedding dress of flowered satin—to walk down the wide staircase in the White House into the Blue Room where she and her husband—nineteenth President of the United States—were to celebrate their silver wedding anniversary.

Outwardly, there was little change in her. After twenty-five years her hair was as black and lustrous as it had been when she was a bride not long out of her classes at Ohio Wesleyan University. Her face was unlined, her brown eyes still gentle in their rather shy expression. As First Lady she was still unassuming, but the years had given her poise and faith in herself.

Intimate friends grouped around the piano in the Blue Room for celebration of the silver wedding anniversary. They were as glad as she that the anniversary had fallen on Sunday. As it was Vice-President Wheeler's turn to select the hymns and old songs of which they never tired, he took his place beside the piano to lead Chief Justice and Mrs. Waite, General Sherman, Secretary Evarts, the Hayeses and the rest of the company in "Hold the Fort" and "The Sweet By and By."

Happy as she was in the small friendly circle at "Sunday evenings," Lucy spared no effort to make official entertainment at the White House attractive. Several days in advance of a state dinner or reception she would give the steward detailed plans for decorations, musical program, usher arrangements and catering service, then personally superintend the final work.

Just a few hours before Rutherford and she were to receive members of the diplomatic corps, she was in the East Room, surrounded by a staff of stewards and clerks, while workmen draped the walls with flags and set plants and flowers in place. All of the staff were listening to her final instructions when Webb Hayes dodged under ladders and over festoons of smilax and hurried up to her.

"Mother, there are two women and a man, Quakers, who insist on seeing you and Father at once so they may deliver a religious message to you," he announced, somewhat breathlessly. "At least fifty people are waiting in Father's office to see him by appointment, and I know you haven't the time to see anyone now. I'll just tell them we have had prayers, that we are all right, and send them away."

For a moment, Lucy was as upset as he. "What shall I do? How can I stop just now?" Then, thoughtfully, "They may have come a long way; we must see them. Ask your father to meet us in the library, Webb."

With the good humor which had led a newspaper editor to describe him as "the President who has the firmness of an Andrew Jackson and the manners of a Chesterfield,"

Rutherford interrupted his work to join Lucy and the visitors. After the greeting there was nothing said for several moments. At last the Friend was ready to speak, and addressed the First Lady and the President as Lucy and Rutherford, then read several passages from the Bible to them. Another long silence followed the reading, broken only when the Friend offered a final prayer.

The morning was dwindling, and there was still much to be done for the reception which Lucy wanted to be one of the year's most successful. She said nothing of the work that faced her, but escorted her grave guests all through the White House, even into her own rooms, pointing out the many historical pieces which she had salvaged from store-rooms in the mansion. Not until they had seen all she thought would interest them did she bid them farewell, and in that cordial goodbye there was no hint that they had taken precious time from one of her busiest days.

Toward the close of the elaborate reception that evening one of the women in the receiving line turned to Lucy. There was a weariness in her voice as she questioned, "Doesn't all this tire you? But I guess it hasn't, for you look as fresh as the flower in your hair. I should collapse after a year as First Lady."

The white camellia in her hair and a silver comb were Lucy's only adornments. Dressed in cream moiré and satin, her arms covered with white gloves, the First Lady was distinguished in a society which competed for attention in its display of jewels and elaborate gowns. Guests called her "clever," "beautiful," and thoroughly understood when they heard that Rutherford had said, "Mrs. Hayes may have no influence with Congress, but she has great influence with me." She was as interested as he in his efforts to promote civil-service reform, as glad as he when he removed troops from the defeated South and gave local control back to states which had seceded; as earnest as he in advancing the welfare of the Indians.

In turn, he supported her decision to prohibit liquor in the White House. So long as he was President and she First Lady, the White House was their home. Lucy had never served liquor at their house in Fremont, Ohio, and she saw no reason why she should desert her principles just because it was customary to serve wine at official dinners in the Executive Mansion. Society forgot enough of its decorum to complain loudly at first, then good-humoredly accepted Lucy's challenge when she asked if people could not be as witty and interesting without wine as with it.

Extensively as she entertained, Lucy kept the management of the White House in her own hands. Her family and her home were still her major interests; so she could not understand the delighted surprise of several women who descended on her one morning at nine o'clock and frankly admired the perfect order of the White House so early in the day. Her greatest enjoyment came from the after-dinner hour each evening when Rutherford and she helped Scott and Fanny, their youngest children, with school lessons, and from the bright mornings when she took them into the garden and, with trowel and clippers, showed them how to care for the flowers she loved.

Each Thanksgiving day she entertained White House clerks and their families at dinner, and after the turkey and pies and cakes took the children into the Red Room where she played whatever games they wanted. At Christmas she received them all in the Red Room and gave them presents she had selected in crowded Washington shops.

Nothing was too much trouble for her if the effort meant happiness to someone, as wounded Union soldiers had learned in the war days when she brought cakes and cookies to them in the hospitals, then stayed to mend their clothes, write letters home, and sing the songs they asked from her. None of them would have been surprised at her concern for the veteran of the War of 1812 who had come to be photographed at the White House. In honor of the occasion, a new uniform had been made for him and delivered directly to the Mansion instead of to the Soldiers' Home. The tailor had neglected to sew on the stripes of the veteran's rank as sergeant, and as the bent old soldier noted the omission all the pride left his eyes. In a moment he was smiling again, for Lucy had taken a "housewife" from her pocket and when the British Minister escorted a party of friends into the room to meet the First Lady of the United States, she was sitting on the floor sewing chevrons on a uniform.

Long after she left the White House, Washington spoke of her, and a sort of legend grew up about her. Servants remembered that they had never been reprimanded while she was First Lady. Attendants at the children's hospital recalled the armfuls of flowers she had sent to the patients almost daily. Political leaders did not forget her interest in woman's suffrage. Social leaders remembered a rather tall, low-voiced, smiling woman with a white camellia in her hair, who challenged them with her simplicity and won them with her grace. At her death, cities throughout the land lowered their flags to half-mast.

Lucretia Rudolph Garfield
(1833–1918)

PENNED in carefully shaded Spencerian writing, the letter opened: "Lucretia, My sister. Please pardon the liberty I take in pointing my pen towards your name—" and so began James Garfield's courtship of Lucretia Rudolph.

Big, restless James was only twenty-two, and Lucretia was just twenty; but they were very grave, very ambitious, and their courtship moved slowly, almost solemnly. As schoolmates at Eclectic Institute—where all students considered themselves "brothers" and "sisters" in the Campbellite faith —in the crossroads village of Hiram, Ohio, their life was secluded and earnest. Occasionally a lecturer visited Hiram, but there was not much thought of recreation in the red brick school in the corn field on the hill. Classes began at five o'clock in the morning with a course in Virgil. After breakfast were sessions of writing copies, grammar, Greek, algebra, then dinner. Algebra was studied again in the afternoon, followed by Latin, geometry, and more Greek. The two hours after supper were given to writing practice, then a glee-club sing, and the school day ended in a two-hour phrenological lecture; before the students went to bed they studied for the next day.

Whenever there was free time, James and other men students cut wood, worked at a carpenter's bench, helped to build houses in the neighborhood, or did odd jobs at the Institute to earn their tuition and board. Lucretia, who lived on the Rudolph farm near Hiram, studied and helped at home in her spare moments.

With their whole hearts and minds James and she were fitting themselves to teach. He threw his great strength and will into learning all that his instructors could teach him; his robust and hungry mind devoured literature, mathematics, and the classics. Lucretia, too, mastered the subjects; but in her method of study she was quiet, keenly observing. James had known her four years before he took the liberty of writing to her; dark and fragile, she had not attracted his attention. In their classes together it was James who led the discussions, while Lucretia listened. His heavily muscled shoulders were too broad for the calico shirt and homespun jacket he wore; his legs too long for the satinet pantaloons that flipped out of his cowhide boots; his light hair too thick to lie smoothly against his head. He was big and he was awkward; but when he spoke in class, everyone turned to listen to his rich voice.

At the informal gatherings of students on free nights he led in the singing while one of the girls played the melopiano or the piano. Lucretia would be there, too, but it was his voice that rollicked in "Don't you remember sweet Alice, Ben Bolt?" In discussions on "life ambitions" and "great achievements," the eager and hearty James commanded listeners.

Lucretia had listened to him for four years before he left Hiram for a visit to Niagara where he realized that he liked to have her, in particular, listen and be with him. They

were not married until 1858 when James had been graduated from Williams College and made president of Eclectic. In those five years of waiting Lucretia had taught school
and continued her own studies, and it was with a feeling of
homecoming that she took up housekeeping in a little cottage on the Institute's campus.

For three years they lived much as they did in their student days when James had rung the bell for classes. Now
someone else tolled the bell, and James was teacher instead
of pupil; but Eclectic was still their world, with teachers
and pupils gathering in their cottage to sing and talk just
as they had talked and sung when James and she were
pupils. In January of 1860 he was elected to the Ohio State
Senate, but he kept the campus cottage at Hiram and discussed his every political plan with Lucretia, in whose judgment he had perfect faith. Even when he went into the field
as Colonel of the Forty-second Ohio, in 1861, his letters to
her described all of his marches and battles, and he inclosed
sketch maps of the battlefields that she might better follow
his movements. Through his letters she watched the "Pray-
ing Colonel"—as some of the soldiers dubbed James because, though he had never been ordained, he had often
preached in Campbellite churches—advance to a brigadier
and become chief-of-staff for General Rosecrans' Army of
the Cumberland.

His letters were not always grim stories of charges and re-
treats, and she smiled when she learned that he had
marched into a Newburgh ballroom and enlisted sixty men
by dramatically describing the fatal merrymaking in Brus-
sels on the eve of Waterloo. Lucretia could see the startled
young men in ruffled shirts, gray and plum-colored tailed
coats, and tight gaiter trousers suddenly deserting their

dancing partners to sign up for service in the Union army.

Frequent letters afforded Lucretia and James but meager companionship. Their days of real comradeship began only after the war when they built a home in Washington, where they stayed during Congressional sessions. While James was at his desk in the House of Representatives, Lucretia schooled the children at home, preparing them in Homer and in Horace, James' favorite Latin writer. During the day she taught them, but every morning at breakfast James became the instructor when he laid a dictionary before his plate and put the children through a pronunciation and definition test. Again at evening he turned to teaching, reading Shakespeare to them, Audubon's studies in natural history, or instructing them in elocution.

At the end of Congressional sessions Lucretia and James were as eager as the children to return to Mentor, Ohio, where the Garfields had bought a farm, Lawnfield. Summer meant swimming and riding and fruit picking to the children. To Lucretia it meant a return to her girlhood life, and weeks of change for James who still liked to ride out to the fields on a hayrack and pitch the dry, dusty grain shoulder high onto the wagon.

It was to the white and red house at Mentor that they went when James was nominated for the presidency of the United States in 1880. From the moment telegraph linemen ran a special wire into the shed which James had made into an office, Lawnfield became a little city and Lucretia became its hostess. Train service was irregular. The nearest hotel was three miles away. Every day, all summer long, newspaper reporters, political leaders, and friends from every part of Ohio drove up to Lawnfield and stayed to talk with James, eat apples from the orchard, wander over the farm, take dinner at the crowded table in the house, and, whenever they could find room, stay overnight. Lucretia forgot that she had ever been a teacher; as she bent over the coal stove to fry and bake, boil and stew, season and baste, she felt as though she had always been a cook. While James worked at his correspondence or conferred with his chief supporter, James G. Blaine of Maine, and gave out interviews, Lucretia was at work to feed the "Plumed Knight" and the army of visitors.

Throughout that summer the political chiefs at Lawnfield directed the campaign which sent James into the White House, and Lucretia prepared to spend her next four years as First Lady.

While in Washington before, she had entertained little. From her life in the capital, however, she knew how important it was to any President that his wife meet the public with cordial generosity, that she preside over the White House with hospitality, that she give a grace to the life there. For the time that a woman is First Lady she is as much a public servant as is the President. Lucretia knew this; so it was just six days after the inauguration that she opened the White House for official entertainment. James watched her as she stood in the receiving line to greet members of the diplomatic corps, and that night he wrote in his diary: "C. ["Crete," his diminutive of "Lucretia"] grows up to every new emergency with fine tact and faultless taste."

Not many weeks after he wrote that tribute, Lucretia met the greatest emergency of all: on July 2 Charles Guiteau shot James as he entered a railroad station in Washington.

In the anxious eighty days that followed, Lucretia grew up to the necessity of keeping faith in the face of death.

For almost three months she surrounded herself and James with a courage that astounded a watching nation. From the time she first knelt beside her wounded husband, through the hours of the strange and frightening journey to New Jersey when a special train sped to a seashore cottage and men pushed the ambulance car by hand to the very door, until the very last moment of James' life she never faltered. In her face the wounded man saw no discouragement, no resignation to defeat, and her faith gave him confidence to carry on his fight. To her he turned when he could not rest; and from her he got comfort and renewed strength. Throughout those last days it was she who was the leader as she tried to guide him back to safety; and James, who had always been the leader, was glad to put his hand in hers.

Ellen Herndon Arthur

(1837–1880)

In the room of Chester A. Arthur, twenty-first President of the United States, was the picture of a youthful woman. She had seen him make his way from a small law practice to leadership in New York politics. She had not lived to see him, at the death of President Garfield, take up leadership of a nation. Each morning, before President Arthur left the room for his office, he placed fresh flowers before her picture.

To New York society Ellen Herndon Arthur had brought the grace of her Southern birth and training. She was born at Culpeper Court House in Virginia, where Herndons had been landholders for almost two hundred years.

Most of her girlhood was spent in Washington and Fredericksburg, Virginia. Later she went to New York, where she met Chester Alan Arthur at the home of a relative. After her marriage in 1859 she was as prominent in philanthropic work as she was in society; seldom was there a concert for charity at which Ellen Arthur, whose voice was an unusually fine contralto, did not sing.

One evening, after she had finished her part on the program of a charity concert, she went out into the street for her carriage. As she stood waiting for her coachman she took the cold that resulted in pneumonia and, three days later, in her death.

Her place as mistress of the White House was taken by Mrs. John McElroy, President Arthur's sister; but it was President Arthur who invested hospitality in the White House with generosity and elegance.

Arthur, whose brown eyes twinkled with sociability, whose tall heavy figure was always so immaculately groomed that the press called him the "Dude President," entertained his own friends almost constantly at dinners and midnight suppers; and no President was more liberally hospitable to the public than he. At the many public receptions, flowers from the presidential conservatories banked the walls of the Red Room, from the thick crimson carpet to the ceiling where copper and bronze stars glinted in the gaslight from heavy chandeliers.

Washington crowded into the White House to enjoy President Arthur's receptions; those were the elegant eighties when America prided itself on etiquette and culture. Early in the life of America, its people had been concerned with winning independence and establishing a nation. From the time of Thomas Jefferson to that of James Buchanan they had busied themselves pushing out the frontiers and developing new country. Next, the Civil War had occupied their energies. Not until after the war and the reconstruction did America really find leisure in which to enjoy itself as a nation. Throughout the early days—in quilting parties, apple parings, log rollings, and husking bees— it had to make play of its work.

So seriously did America take its social life in the newfound leisure of the 1880's that it made work of its play.

There was a heavy splendor of dress and manners. For formal dinners damask-covered tables were set with crystal and glass; then decorated with plateau mirrors, gilt candelabra bearing shaded candles and many flowers. Ladies wore wine-colored velvets trimmed in Pompadour brocade, or cardinal satin with court trains embroidered in gold, or terra-cotta satin ornamented with flowered brocade and lace, or marine-blue velvet and long trains trimmed in iridescent bugles. Pomaded gentlemen, dressed in the rich black of evening clothes and Inverness capes, escorted them to cotillions and suppers; to the theater to see Dion Boucicault of the flashing eyes and imperious voice; to the concert halls to hear Joseffy or Adelina Patti, who was guaranteed four thousand dollars a night.

Plays, concerts, suppers, and balls were given in the grand manner to grand dames and gentlemen; but the grand manner was at its grandest in the White House. Against a background of flowers and music, candlelight and clear crystal, was gathered the brilliance of the fashionable eighties; and there was, in it all, a courtly, a rich dignity which Ellen Herndon Arthur would have been proud to see.

Frances Folsom Cleveland
(1864–1947)

"THREE thousand handshakes in two hours—three thousand smiles," exclaimed a friend as she watched young Mrs. Grover Cleveland greet the last guests at a public reception in the White House.

For two hours the First Lady had been giving her ungloved hand to twenty-five people a minute, and her greeting to the last in line was as cordial as it had been to the first. Her voice and her smile gave welcome to each, and she won the allegiance of all. No one could meet her, even briefly, without sensing her friendliness.

Not since the time of Dolley Madison had a First Lady so captured the fancy of the nation. From the moment she stood in the Blue Room beneath a wedding bell of roses for her marriage to Grover Cleveland, twenty-second President of the United States, she became a symbol of romance. Everywhere throughout the country people eagerly read that the President's twenty-two-year-old bride was a graduate of Wells College; that she had been his ward since the death of her father Oscar Folsom, who had been Mr. Cleveland's law partner in Buffalo; that she was slim and dark haired and very lovely to look at. They liked to think of her—young

Frances Folsom, twenty-two years old, married Grover Cleveland

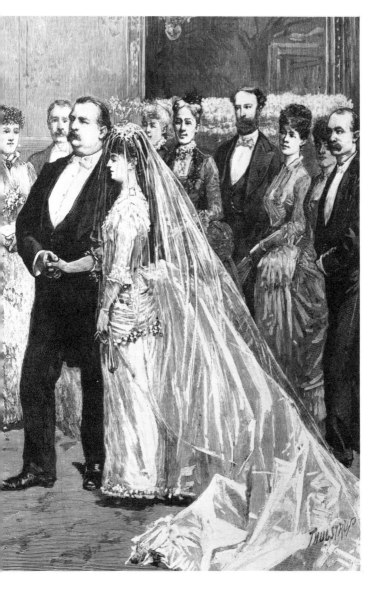

in the White House and became the youngest First Lady.

and radiant in a bridal gown of corded satin draped with India silk and banded by orange blossoms, her dark hair misted by a veil of silk tulle—being married to the President of the United States in a White House bright with orchids, lilies-of-the-valley, and red and white roses.

They read all they could of her and liked all they read; but they wondered if so young a First Lady could meet the standard that women of far wider social experience had set for mistresses of the White House. They need not have been concerned. The young First Lady not only measured up to the traditional standard, but surpassed it to set one of her own.

As soon as she returned to Washington after a brief honeymoon at Deer Park, residents of Washington ordered their carriages and drove to the White House to leave their visiting cards for her. Of all the women in Washington's official life Mrs. Cleveland alone, as wife of the President, was free from the obligation of making or returning calls. Ladies of the Cabinet received on Wednesdays, wives of the Senators on Thursdays, and wives of Representatives often grouped together to receive guests on stated days. Then everyone bustled about to all parts of the city three or four afternoons a week to return those calls and to make others. No other city in the United States made such demands on wives of public officials; but even novices in the social life of the capital became skilled in paying from thirty to forty calls in an afternoon.

Instead of there being but one reception day at the White House, the Mansion was opened to the public on Wednesdays, Fridays, and Saturdays. Crowds were so great that military aides frequently had to halt the line to let Mrs. Cleveland rest for a moment against a chair or sofa before introductions and handshaking began again. Then the procession resumed its march from hall to Red Room into Blue Room to meet the First Lady, to catch her smile and see what she wore, then out through Green Room and East Room and into the hall again, remembering her firm handclasp and the grace of violets at the belt of her lavender gown.

Throughout the season there were receptions for the diplomatic corps, the judiciary, Congress, and the Army and Navy; then the round of dinners and musicals. During the day people wandered through the Mansion and democratically made themselves at home in the stately East Room. Except for a few private rooms reserved for the President and his family on the second floor, the White House was truly the "People's House"; and for three years young Mrs. Cleveland was the people's hostess. Then on March 4, 1889, when Benjamin Harrison succeeded Mr. Cleveland as President, she returned to private life. After a last look to see that the Executive Mansion was in order for Mrs. Harrison, that luncheon was prepared for her and flowers were on the table, she said goodbye to the staff.

Just four years later she moved in again, greeted all the servants by name, and resumed the duties of First Lady as though she had been gone but a day. As Mr. Cleveland was the only President to be re-elected after a defeat, she was the only First Lady to return to the White House after an absence of four years.

The President and Mrs. Cleveland had not long been back in the White House when they felt the lash of gossip. In their four years of absence from public life they had not changed. President Cleveland was still the vigorous reformer whose fight against corrupt politics had caused people to

"love him for the enemies he made." Mrs. Cleveland was
still the young and lovely woman whom everyone had admired because she was as lovely as she looked. The change
was not in them. It was in the public which, after it re-
elected Grover Cleveland to the presidency, found fault
with almost every measure he indorsed and childishly
blamed him for a widespread business panic.

Just as Mrs. Cleveland shared the honor of his position
with him, so had she to share the burden of it. The public
wanted to know not only every official move made by the
President, but it wanted to pass judgment on every move
made in his private life. When his wife tried to protect
Ruth, born just before Mr. Cleveland was re-elected, from
the crowds who sought to see and caress her, the public at
once made up its mind that there was some sinister reason
for secluding the baby. When the President did not accompany Mrs. Cleveland to the theater, the public decided that
there was violent discord between them. The public decided,
and the public was loud in its decisions; and President
Cleveland was grim when he wrote to a friend, "Don't ever
run for the Presidency," explaining, "a sensitive man cannot
be happy as President."

In those last years in the White House Mrs. Cleveland
learned that the public feels privileged to dishonor those
whom it has honored. It was a hard lesson and a strange
one. Nevertheless, she tucked violets, fresh and graceful,
into her belt and stood at her post in the Blue Room, giving
her hand and smile to a public that only then forgot to
criticize. One by one those in the long line filed up to the
First Lady. And one by one they went on again, and were
not so eager then to take part in gossiping about her. Even
those who had talked loudest and hardest could not forget

her smile, a grave smile now, and the bravery of her eyes.

In June of 1886 she had come to them as a bride in white satin and orange blossoms to take her place in a White House magnificent with lilies and orchids. She had made herself their friend, and they became her friends. In March of 1889 she had gone away and then returned to find them hostile, petulant, and finally cruel. It was they who had changed, not she; so she won them back again with a grave gentleness. When in 1897 she said goodbye to them for the last time as mistress of the White House, she again carried their friendship with her; but she alone knew how fully she had paid for the title she had won, "the most popular of First Ladies."

After those last four years in the White House she welcomed the informality and fellowship with which the university town of Princeton, New Jersey, accepted the former President and his family, as they took up residence in their new home, Westland. Students marched up their walk after big games to cheer Grover Cleveland while he congratulated Princeton on its victories. They recorded the birth of Richard Folsom Cleveland on the campus bulletin board, heralding him as a future member of the Orange and Black varsity. Mrs. Cleveland relished their buoyant enthusiasm. She was content to be known as the mother of the future Princeton football center; yet thousands throughout the country, even after her marriage to Thomas J. Preston— following the death of Grover Cleveland—continued to think of her as Frances Cleveland. To them she was the ideal First Lady.

Caroline Scott Harrison
(1832–1892)

THROUGH the streets of downtown Indianapolis surged a
laughing, singing crowd of excited men, who quieted only
when a reporter or copy boy raced out from a newspaper
office to shout: "Latest returns from New York show votes
turn to Harrison!" or "Cleveland leads in Pennsylvania!"
For hours the Harrison men shifted from cheers to grim
silence, then again to cheers and swoops of their lighted
torches as news favored Republicans, Democrats, and again
Harrison Republicans.

While crowds stormed newspaper and telegraph offices,
nothing was going on in the Indianapolis home of the Har-
risons to indicate that any of the family had a particular
interest in the election. Rather early in the evening Caroline
Harrison quietly observed that she was a little tired after
her day of work at the Indianapolis orphan asylum, and
thought she would go to bed. Her husband rose from the
chair in which he had been reading, and agreed that her
idea sounded very good to him, too.

"But, General, don't you want to hear the final returns
and know if you are elected President?" asked Harrison's
son-in-law, James McKee, in surprise. "The *Journal* is going

to telephone us as soon as the final vote is known."

Pleasantly, but with the firmness which had so often snapped raw recruits to attention when he commanded a brigade of Sherman's Army of the West, General Harrison answered: "No, James, I really think Mrs. Harrison's idea of going to sleep is a better one. What good would it do if I were to sit up and get the returns? Should I be defeated, my staying up all night would do no good; should I win, it is better that I be rested and fresh for the activity of to-morrow."

Red light of torches streaked the night as Republicans celebrated their victory; but they celebrated without the presence of their hero. General Harrison, President-elect of the United States, did not waken until he was called at seven o'clock in the morning to receive congratulations of enthusiasts massed in the street before his home.

Mrs. Harrison and he took their places in the White House with the same calm practicality in which they had worked to civic leadership in Indianapolis. From the day they had first met, when Harrison, a grandson of William Henry Harrison, was a student at Miami University and Caroline a pupil at Oxford Female Institute, they had been interested in education and social service. They were married in 1854 while Harrison was still studying law.

Her six years in Washington while the General served in the Senate, (1881–1887), had acquainted Mrs. Harrison with social life in the capital; so she was prepared for her duties as mistress of the White House. Few First Ladies had brought to the Executive Mansion such a serene beauty of age as did she. Her hair, white and soft, was waved back off her ears; her eyes were full and wide; her mouth, firm and clear-cut; and when visitors were ushered into the Red

Room to meet her, they thought the graceful, restful setting of open fireplace, richly grained furniture, and mellow sunlight was a perfect background for their hostess. Had the First Lady been given her choice of setting, however, she would probably have returned to Indianapolis and gone as fast as a hack would carry her to the city orphan asylum and resumed her work in its administration.

Much as she appreciated her honor as First Lady, she regretted the restrictions which the etiquette of her position placed upon her. No longer could she give whole days to working on charity cases, for she had to be ready at almost any hour to receive visitors into the White House. What she felt to be her most valued work was ended when she became First Lady; and she agreed with General Harrison as he looked at the White House, on returning from a walk, and said, "There is my prison."

Like him, too, the little time she reserved from her public duties she gave to her grandson, Benjamin Harrison McKee, whom everyone but his parents and grandparents called "Baby McKee." It was for nationally famous Baby McKee that the first Christmas tree was set up in the White House. All afternoon of that December 24, gardeners worked in the library over the Blue Room; but immediately after dinner the President of the United States joined them to help decorate the tree, while the First Lady of the Land stretched and stooped to fill the branches with presents.

In spite of all their efforts to protect Ben from publicity, reporters stalked the Executive Mansion to supply newspapers with feature stories on what Baby McKee wore, etc, did, said. Almost as much space was given to President Harrison's chase of Ben in a runaway goat cart as to his work in promoting civil-service reform or effecting the

Bering Sea arbitration. Even at the presidential summer cottage in the Pennsylvania mountains, reporters stationed themselves to watch Ben greet his guests at a children's hop when young girls in plaid silk, and their brushed and shining partners, uncomfortable in tight suits, bobbed and turned in polkas and schottisches.

As the Harrison administration neared a close, newspapers grew harsh in their treatment of the President. During his term of office he had strengthened America's position as a world power, and under his guidance domestic industry greatly developed; but he was a statesman and not a politician. Because he made no concessions to political leaders, he found himself unpopular, and the press of the day delighted in harassing him, pointing out that "Kid Glove" Harrison was a "human iceberg." He did not mind the editorial attacks so much for himself as for Mrs. Harrison, who could not help crying at the bitterest of them. For her sake he was glad that his term of office was almost expired.

She was not prepared for the news he brought one day when he declared that he was going to run again for the presidency; but she only looked away for a moment, then quietly asked, "Why, General? Why, when it has been so hard for you here?"

"If Blaine and some of those who I thought were my political friends had not turned upon me, as they have done, I should retire from office with no thought of allowing my name to be used in the nominations. But no Harrison has ever run from a fight, Caroline, and there is going to be a fight."

Into that fight went the Harrison who would not run away; and the woman, who earlier had wanted nothing more than to run away, encouraged him. Others made speeches for him, others got him the nomination of his party, others carried banners and canvassed for political support; but she heartened him with faith and understanding. When she became ill, and rest and quiet were ordered for her, she still wanted to hear progress of his campaign, still wanted to do her share to help him win. Her thought was to regain strength as soon as possible and once more take her place at his side, but she could not overcome the illness. Had she lived, she would have stood beside him in defeat, a little glad that "defeat" meant they were to go home again.

Ida Saxton McKinley

(1844–1907)

HER European holiday had been the happiest sort of graduation present. She was quite sure of this; but, all the same,
she was glad to be back home. It had been a novelty to go
up to New York to school, and it had been exciting to visit
London and Paris; but there was something about walking
down the familiar streets of Canton, Ohio, and hearing
welcomes from half the town that brought a pleasure which
one never got from all the strolls in the Bois de Boulogne.

Even as she seated herself in a clerk's chair, fastened a
pair of paper cuffs over the sleeves of her blouse, and poked
rather indefinitely at a pad of figures, she told herself again
that it was nice to be home. She was not sure that she was
going to like the banking business, but she was determined
to try. That her father was president of the bank did not
seem to make it easier to find her way through the maze of
figures on the pad nor to feel confident that she understood
terms of discounts and renewals.

Morning after morning the stiff chair, paper cuffs, freshly
sharpened pencils, and columns of figures awaited her at
the bank; and it was not long before she fastened the cuffs
with brisk efficiency and talked familiarly of mortgages and

farm loans. When she earned the promotion, her father advanced her to position of cashier and was satisfied that his ambition of fitting her to earn her own way was fulfilled. But to Canton came a young veteran of the Civil War, William McKinley, whose gallantry under fire had won him the brevet of major at twenty-two; and William Mc-Kinley's ambitions were to become a successful lawyer and to win Ida Saxton for his wife.

He was reasonably certain that he would attain the first; he was very diffident about venturing for the second. Ida Saxton, as the daughter of a prosperous banker, was accustomed to more than a young lawyer could offer her at the start of his career. Young and happy, she carried her head high and a little to the side, and there was a lilt in her voice. As her father looked at her, he smiled his pleasure at her buoyant independence. As William McKinley looked at her, surrounded by young men, he frowned and thought that sometimes it was easier to have courage on the battle-field than in the ballroom.

At last he did venture, and he won. They were married on January 25, 1871, and began their life together in the happiest sort of circumstances. Mr. Saxton had given them a home as a wedding present. Major McKinley was firmly established in a good law practice and was already earning a name for himself in public office. Mrs. McKinley, spirited and young and beautiful, was a leader in the friendly social life of the town. To Canton, Major McKinley and his wife represented good fortune and happiness.

That was in 1871. Five years later, at the death of her two children, Mrs. McKinley became an invalid, able to walk only with the assistance of a cane and supported by the arm of her husband or a friend. She could no longer go out as she had once done, but Canton came to her. Every day, in a sitting room bright and fragrant with bowls of roses, she was surrounded by friends, just as she had been at parties before her marriage.

Although she was seldom without visitors, she was completely dependent upon Major McKinley for her happiness, and he did not fail her. As he advanced in public life, he had to travel throughout the state to make political speeches. Whenever he spoke in the larger towns, where he thought hotel accommodations would be suitable for her, he took her with him. If he were to stump the villages and farming country, he arranged his program so that no matter where he was, he could return to her for the weekend. Throughout his two terms as Governor of Ohio they lived in a Columbus hotel near the capitol; and each morning, as he entered the statehouse grounds, he turned to face the hotel window from which she was watching, lifted his hat, and bowed to her. Each afternoon at three o'clock, no matter who was with him or what business was at hand, he went to the window of his office and waved a handkerchief to her as she waited for his sign of thoughtfulness.

When they went into the White House, in 1897, he quietly ignored the custom that placed the President at one end of the table, for official dinners, and the First Lady at the other. The McKinleys entertained extensively, and the President seated his wife at his right hand. Later, in the drawing-room, he stood beside her chair.

Even before McKinley was inaugurated, President Cleveland had warned him that war with Spain was inevitable; but the new President did all in his power to avoid the conflict. He devoted his first months in office to keeping the United States from war. The strain and responsibility wore

him down; and, as he talked with a confidential adviser one evening about the sinking of the battleship *Maine* in Havana harbor, there was despair in his voice.

Congress, he said, was trying to force the country into war, and the country was not prepared to fight. Neither ammunition nor men were available; but because the President avoided aggression he was accused of cowardice.

His head was bent in his hands as he talked, and he seemed to be lost in his own unhappiness. Suddenly he lifted his head and spoke, not of war nor of a bellicose Congress. He said, "But I must return to Mrs. McKinley at once. She is among strangers." Back into the Blue Room he went where visitors to the White House were gathered for a musical, and he took his place beside her.

Three years later, on the afternoon of September 6, 1901, when he was to receive the public in the Exposition Hall at Buffalo, he sent her back to the home of their host so that she would not be tired by the throng. He promised to return to her as soon as he could, and she was waiting there for him when Leon Czolgosz crowded up to him in the Exposition Hall and shot him. As the President fell to the floor he pointed to Czolgosz, whom the maddened crowd had seized, and said, "Don't let them hurt him." Then he whispered to his secretary, "My wife—be careful how you tell her—oh, be careful!" To those around him it seemed as though his wounds did not matter to him; he suffered only in the thought that he was to bring sorrow to her whom he had always protected.

On September 14 he died; and she returned to the home in Canton which, thirty years before, they had entered together. But, for her, home without him at her side seemed a place among strangers.

Edith Carow Roosevelt

(1861–1948)

Summer, 1875. Spray stung their faces and smarted their eyes; but the sun-browned boy and girl only flung back their heads to shake it off, as their squat little rowboat slapped into troughs and swooped again to white crests. The boy pulled his oars in a quick easy rhythm, enjoying the choppy bay water; and the girl, wind and sun beating into her face, shared his zest. He was Theodore Roosevelt and she was Edith Kermit Carow. He was seventeen and she was fourteen.

Summer, 1887. Spray whipped into their faces and spattered into the boat; but the sun-browned young woman only tucked her skirts round the picnic lunch and the volumes of Thackeray, and smiled as she wiped the water from her cheeks. The sun-browned young man grinned as he pulled quickly, easily on his oars and drove the boat out into the Sound. They were Mr. and Mrs. Theodore Roosevelt, home after several months of travel following their marriage in London the year before.

Home was Sagamore Hill, the many-chimneyed house that looked out from meadows and woodland to Oyster Bay and the Sound. On Sagamore, "Chieftain's Hill" as the

From left to right: Theodore Roosevelt holding Archie, Ted standing by Alice, Kermit and Ethel with Mrs. Roosevelt

Indians called it in the long-ago days of their chief Sagamore Mohannis, fields and woods flowered with trailing arbutus, anemones, dogwood, and locust, and perky bobolinks sang in meadows. Sagamore meant long cross-country tramps and rides, rowing and swimming in the bay, logs burning across open fireplaces. Later, as the children were born, it became a whole world of fun and experience into which young Ted, Kermit, Ethel, Archie, and Quentin adventured.

They clambered and wriggled and leaped, true to the motto of "Over or through, never around" set by their father, on the obstacle races that led them into the barn, through the hay, over fences, or along sandy Cooper's Bluff and into the tide. They hunted flowers and tamed pets. Into the nursery they brought their guinea pigs, flying squirrels, kangaroo rats, Josiah the badger, and Sailor Boy the huge

Chesapeake Bay retriever. The black bear cub, Jonathan Edwards, and the two ponies, General Grant and the calico Algonquin, seemed happier outside with Susan the cow.

Guinea pigs squealed when ardent young masters hugged them too tightly. Pet rats scurried in and out of corners while squirrels rustled busily across the floor, and a dog or two yipped joyously as it raced a small boy or girl down the hall. Four little boys and one little girl, restless with energy, explored and hunted as a comradely father led them in the free, wholehearted life he so loved.

Mother, too, joined them on cross-country rides and at splashes on the bay shore. She enjoyed all they enjoyed, but she never let the romp get out of hand. When they came to her with their scratches and bumps she patched them deftly and gently.

At night they would curl up in the nursery, each in his favorite knot of a position, while Mother read *Alice in Wonderland, Brer Rabbit, Robin Hood,* or *Voodoo Tales;* or listen to Father's reading of *Guy Mannering* and *The Last of the Mohicans,* or to stories of his roundup and hunting days in Dakota ranch lands. As he talked to them they could almost see the weathered punchers riding herd on the Little Missouri; roping horses with lariats that whirred and snaked through the air to encircle plunging heads; mastering, without pulling leather, bronchos that bucked and "sun-fished" like outlaws; striding up to the chuck wagon, their high-heeled boots making them roll a little as they walked; yearning a bit round the campfire as they munched a supper of bread and bacon from tin plates; rolling up in blankets for the night with their saddles for pillows.

When Father became President of the United States and

Mother First Lady of the Land, they remained the comrades they had been to the children at Sagamore. Ted and Kermit were at Groton; but Ethel, Archie, and Quentin simply transferred the calico Algonquin, guinea pigs, dogs, boats, kites, and treasures from Sagamore to the White House. The obstacle walks were made in Rock Creek Park. Mother fitted the former cabinet room for a nursery, and there she comforted them when they tumbled and skinned their knees and knuckles. At night she read to them in the library while Tom Quartz the kitten plagued Jack the dog, who preferred to drowse at the fireside.

In his office hours, Father was President of the United States and wielded "the big stick" over belligerent businessmen and legislators, put through construction of the Panama Canal, and won the Nobel Peace Prize for his settlement of the Russo-Japanese War. It was Father, too, who formally named the Executive Mansion "The White House," a name that had previously been in only occasional use. Mother, although she did not employ a housekeeper, so dexterously managed the White House that her day, too, was divided into home life and "office hours." Throughout breakfast, the favorite meal of the day, when Archie and Ethel and Quentin related adventures and expounded their own particular theories—with vigorous and frank rebuttals from each other—she was Mother. At 9:45 o'clock, immediately after her walk with Theodore Roosevelt in the garden before he went to his office, she became First Lady.

To conserve her time, she engaged a social secretary, the first to be employed in the White House. That was the efficient move of an executive. Her next move was that of a skilled hostess: for her guest list she unobtrusively divided Washington into the political group, the "inner set," and the circle whose interests and tastes were like her own. For each of these groups she gave carefully arranged parties.

As neither the President nor she expected to save anything from his salary, they decided they might just as well spend it on the entertainment which tradition demands of those in the White House. A contract was given to a caterer to serve state dinners for eight dollars a plate; so Mrs. Roosevelt was free of the need to supervise details of arrangement. At the President's wish, Congress made an appropriation for renovating the White House and for building a new structure to house the executive offices. The enlarged White House was then seldom without guests; but it was so perfectly managed that even the President's sisters made appointments with the social secretary if they wanted to see Mrs. Roosevelt during the day.

At luncheons the President talked with each of the guests in his individual fields of interest. Conversation leaped from the wit of Secretary Elihu Root to the jovial humor of Secretary Taft—back and forth from state questions to anecdote. But it was the President who mingled discussions of birds, brief and incisive analyses of political questions, unexpected quotations from Kipling and Swinburne, descriptions of throws he had just learned from his Japanese wrestling instructors, recollections of his Rough-Rider days, and sudden references to Euripides or the lore of the Nibelungenlied.

They all enjoyed the White House—President and First Lady, Father and Mother, Ethel and Archie and Quentin. On nights when there were no receptions or musicals, there were pillow fights with Father and readings with Mother. Even when formal entertainment barred races down the hall—while Quentin pounded on the pianola to spur the contestants—there was still fun for them in concerts and garden parties, for each hoped that Mother would wear the dress he or she liked best.

They all enjoyed anything they did together, and not until the children were grown and started on their own lives did Mother, after the death of Theodore Roosevelt, leave them to find her own world of adventure.

To France and Italy she went first, revisiting Paris and Genoa and reading about Pinocchio in Italian. Finally, she flew to London before she sailed for Cape Town and a picnic on the rocks near the lighthouse. Another visit to Brazil and a trip around the world completed what she called "the odyssey of a grandmother."

She went to the far places that called to her; journeying from white beach to jungle and from lands of shrines and temple bells to snow-drifted barrens; and returned home again to "Chieftain's Hill" where a many-chimneyed house looked out from meadow and woodland to the familiar waters of the bay and the Sound. Near her were the homes of the children. At Cove Neck lived Kermit; at Cold Spring Harbor, Archie; at Oyster Bay, Ethel, who was married to Richard Derby; at Sagamore Hill, Theodore junior. Quentin alone, "the little boy of the White House," was not there; his plane had been shot down in World War I.

There, near the bay she read and studied and wrote the history of her mother's New England family. She had vagabonded, after her work as Mother was done, and she was home again. Before her, beyond field and woodland, lay the bay and the Sound. She had adventured in jungles and upon mountains, but always she had come back to the sea. "All of my journeys," she wrote, "begin and end with the ocean. . . . I have 'salt water around my heart.'"

Helen Herron Taft

(1861–1943)

As Helen Taft stepped from her room in Malacañan palace, the Philippines, after the typhoon had blown itself out, and watched two feet of water swish over the marble floor of the entrance hall, she smiled as though she were enjoying a joke on herself.

She had closed her very comfortable home in Cincinnati and journeyed with three young children more than nine thousand miles out to the Orient and down the China Sea to the Islands, because she was eager to go to new lands and meet new adventures. New lands she had seen and new adventures she had met, and now here she was housed in a palace into which typhoons hurled torrents of rain. But, flooded or not, a palace was still a palace, and she loved living in it.

Mrs. Taft did not always wait for something to happen. When monotony threatened to dull her days, she livened them by making things happen. Her childhood in the gray brick Herron house in Cincinnati was full enough of school and play and music lessons to satisfy even her agile mind and imagination. There were coasting parties on William Howard Taft's bobsled, and amateur theatricals and charades. Suddenly, Helen Herron decided that she must give up what she called a "frivolous life" and devote herself to "useful works." She became a schoolteacher. Then she started a salon, harking back to the days of the French Empire when talent and wit met in drawing rooms to exchange ideas on art, government, and philosophy. Among the guests was William Taft who in later years pointed out to her that the salon gave rise to two marriages, one of them, in 1886, being their own. He wondered if the founders had not had more than intellectual interests, but Mrs. Taft disclaimed any such intrigue.

After a wedding trip abroad they made their home in Cincinnati where Mrs. Taft organized the Cincinnati Orchestra association and took part in many civic movements. Interested as she was in her active life there, she hesitated not a moment when Mr. Taft came to her one day and asked her if she wanted to go to the Philippines. "Yes, of course," she answered, then thought to ask why they were going. That was in January of 1900; Spain had recently surrendered the Philippines to the United States, and the Islands were still under martial rule. President McKinley appointed Mr. Taft head of a commission to establish a civil government there; so in April Mrs. Taft bundled her three children into traveling clothes and set off across the continent to meet her husband in San Francisco.

When they landed from the army transport ship in Japan they learned that they were expected at an audience with the Emperor and Empress. Mrs. Taft had not prepared to make a court appearance, but with the ingenuity of the lover of adventure she called in an Oriental seamstress to remake an evening gown into a high-necked court dress overnight. Between fittings she practiced bending in the low bows prescribed by Eastern etiquette, then presented herself at the court of the Son of Heaven as poised as though she had spent weeks getting ready for the audience.

After a summer in Yokohama, in a bungalow across from a Buddhist temple where priests chanted all day long and beat upon their wooden drums, she joined Mr. Taft in Manila. In a tiny victoria drawn by Philippine ponies, they drove over the Bridge of Spain and along a moat to a spreading house where the bay shone through windows made of pearl shell. The house was old and worn, but it was cool and it had a wide veranda which overlooked the bay, and Mrs. Taft was reluctant to leave it when the appointment of Mr. Taft to the governorship of the Islands necessitated a move to the Malacañan palace.

In their smaller home, it had been the evening coolness from the bay which pleased Mrs. Taft when she entertained a dinner party on the veranda, while a native orchestra played beneath swinging Japanese lanterns. Even though Malacañan was a palace and she felt a tingle of excitement at living in it, she was sure that she was going to miss the bay. The first night, she stepped out on the open veranda at Malacañan and looked across the Pasig River to rice fields where lanterns glowed in thatched huts, saw the Southern stars high and white above her, and heard the wind's faint stir in the bamboos along the river's edge. She knew she would not miss the bay.

She was now First Lady of the Philippines. While her husband, as the first American governor of the Islands, worked at bettering conditions in the Philippines, she did all that she could to show the Filipinos that their new American guardians were their friends. Each week she inserted an "at home" notice in the newspapers for all to see, and announced to her Chinese cook, "Reception Wednesday, Ah Sing." Then, sure that placid Ah Sing would return to his kitchen kingdom and bake hundreds of little cakes, she made her announcement to the six houseboys, who tied banana leaves to their feet and skated zealously up and down the palace rooms as they polished floors for reception day. When the floors and heavy carved furniture shone, the First Lady was ready to receive guests in her palace.

They came gladly, two thousand of them, Americans and Filipinos to visit with the First Lady and to eat Ah Sing's cakes and fruit tarts. The Americans—government officials with their wives, and schoolteachers, suddenly thrust into a strange country thousands of miles from home—were lonely, and the Filipinos, who had so recently been given their freedom from Spain, were shy. Both welcomed Mrs. Taft's informal and friendly receptions. The Filipinos, almost as bewildered by their liberty as they had been by their subjection to Spain, quickly responded to the interest of the Governor and his lady. They felt that they had two great friends—one in the government offices, the other who received them so kindly in her palace.

In 1902 President Roosevelt offered Governor Taft an appointment to the bench of the Supreme Court. The Filipinos protested his leaving them, and filled Manila with signs of "*Queremos Taft,*" "We want Taft." He declined the appointment in order to continue his work in the Islands; nor did he leave the Philippines until 1903, when he became Secretary of War in President Roosevelt's cabinet.

Once in Washington Mrs. Taft was scarcely settled as a "cabinet lady" and started on the required calls and receptions, dinner parties in and dinner parties out, when Secre-

The Tafts with their children Charles, Helen, and Robert

tary Taft had to investigate the Panama Canal situation. Mrs. Taft accompanied him. Down they went to Colón, where they saw in rusted and twisted machinery the defeated efforts of the French to cut a canal through the jungle.

At the end of the Congressional session she left Washington for a summer in Europe, then joined Secretary Taft in Cuba where he had gone to settle political affairs in the tottering republic. After proclaiming a provisional American government there, he made himself provisional governor; so Mrs. Taft presided over the palace at Havana for three days as First Lady of Cuba. While foreign diplomats, Cubans, and officers of the United States Army and Navy attended her first reception, the municipal band in the palace park played Spanish music and American ragtime.

Mrs. Taft was getting accustomed to being First Lady here and there, East and West; yet on the day her husband was inaugurated President of the United States no one was more delightfully excited than she. Her eleven-year-old son Charlie took a copy of *Treasure Island* with him to the inaugural ceremonies in case his father's speech should bore him; but she was on the alert to catch every word of the President's address, which interested even Charlie so that he forgot his favorite author. As soon as Mr. Taft took the oath of office and kissed the Bible handed him by Chief Justice Fuller a signal was flashed from the dome of the Capitol to the navy yard, a mile distant, and a ten-inch gun cracked out the presidential salute.

At the close of his inaugural address, President Taft left the Capitol for the return drive to the White House. The new First Lady then set a precedent, and later confessed that she enjoyed it perhaps more than any other of the day's happenings. Mr. Roosevelt had announced that he would not ride back to the White House with his successor; so Mrs. Taft, dressed in springlike purple satin, seated herself in the carriage and, for the first time in history, a President's wife shared the honor of the return drive to the Executive Mansion.

Lunch booths, toy hawkers, side-show tents and temporary grandstands lined Pennsylvania Avenue where seats were sold at prices ranging from 25¢ to $5. Windows in hotels and business houses brought from $25 to five hundred dollars; and the committee on arrangements had asked women to refrain from wearing the modish "Merry Widow" hats, and to cover their heads instead with toques or scarfs. Overnight a blizzard drenched the bunting and decorations, tore down telegraph wires, and buried the capital in snow; but just after the inauguration, skies cleared, and enthusiastic crowds hurried from shelter to see the President and First Lady return to the White House.

From a reviewing stand at the White House the President and Mrs. Taft watched the inaugural parade. In the line of march were sixty bands and thirty thousand people; and when President Taft had stood in the reviewing stand until the last had passed out of sight, he could think of nothing more pleasant than to sit down and rest before going to the inaugural ball.

Mrs. Taft left him and set out to explore their new home, although she was not at all a stranger to the White House. At seventeen she had been the guest there of Lucy Webb Hayes. Later, when Mr. Taft was Secretary of War, she had gone there weekly to meet with Mrs. Roosevelt's "parlor cabinet." But for the first time the White House was home to her. She stood over the brass seal set in the floor of the

After the Inauguration, Helen Taft established a precedent when she rode from the Capitol with her husband.

entrance hall and read "The Seal of the President of the United States." She made a quick tour through the Blue bedroom and the Pink, the library and the President's study, and into the presidential suite from which she looked out over the White House gardens, past the Washington monument beyond the Potomac to the red hills of Virginia. She had been First Lady in two palaces, and now the White House was home.

As she drove about Washington in the first White House automobile she regretted that the city did not have a place like the Luneta. In the Islands, all Manila went out every evening to the Luneta, a park on the bay shore, for public concerts. Potomac Park, she thought, could be fashioned into a semblance of the Luneta; so she arranged for the building of a bandstand and for concerts each Wednesday and Saturday. On the opening day she knew her plan was a success, as thousands crowded the park for the first concert by the Marine band.

Washington so enthusiastically welcomed that idea that she at once thought of adding another bit of beauty to the city. At her suggestion White House gardeners set out cherry trees in Potomac Park. Tokyo became interested in the First Lady's efforts to give Washington an annual cherry-blossom festival, and sent three thousand trees to be planted in the city.

Washington now cherishes the cloud of pink and white blooms as its very own spring beauty; but it is a beauty made possible by Helen Taft and her love of adventure.

Ellen Axson Wilson
(1860–1914)

EASILY, confidently she sketched the clustered pines and the red lane under their cool shadows. The light was changing, and Ellen Axson wanted to catch the fullness of the shadows; but even as she worked in the fleeing sunlight there was a smooth and unhurried rhythm to her drawing. Her girlhood had been spent in Rome, Georgia, where her father, the Reverend Samuel E. Axson, was minister of the Presbyterian Church; but now that she had finished school there at Shorter College she was going up to study at the Art League in New York. She had set her heart on a career in painting.

For a year or two she thought of little else. Down in Baltimore, at Johns Hopkins University, slender serious Woodrow Wilson was thinking of little but his graduate studies in history and political economy. The young artist and the young student had known each other in Georgia, but each was ambitious for a career; and it was not until 1885, when Woodrow Wilson received his doctorate from Johns Hopkins, that the artist forsook her own ambition to help him on the way to his. When she made that decision they returned South for the wedding. They were mar-

Ellen Wilson planned the White House rose garden, including the President's rose-lined walk.

ried on June 24 in the house of her birth, the manse of the Independent Presbyterian Church at Savannah, Georgia, of which her grandfather, the Reverend I. S. K. Axson, was pastor.

In the autumn they went north to Pennsylvania to Bryn Mawr College. Dr. Wilson began his career as teacher, and Ellen Axson Wilson began a career of her own. Her brilliant husband was shy, keenly sensitive, and she placed herself as a buffer between him and the irritations of daily life. His reserved manner kept people at a distance before they noted the candor of his fine gray eyes; but the welcome of Ellen Wilson's Southern voice held them until they found friendliness in her husband's smile. He wanted friendship, but he could not break down his reserve, the wall of self-control. His wall held him a lonely prisoner; Ellen Wilson, who knew that to make friends, one must be friendly, brought people to him.

In 1890 they went to Princeton where he became professor of jurisprudence and political economy. She planned their home in the university town, taught her three daughters—Margaret, Eleanor, Jessie—and fashioned their clothes, and smoothed the way through the politics and jealousies of faculty life for Woodrow Wilson. People whom she knew he should meet, she had him meet. Those who would take his time for nothing, she met and left him free to read and study. She joined few clubs and entered few civic movements because she wished to be ready whenever he needed her. Her career, as she saw it, was to keep him fit for his—and his led to the White House.

Even there she surrounded him with the quiet home life that had rested him in their university days. Gladly she sacrificed the momentary pleasure of an inaugural ball. Not only was pageantry distasteful to him, but they had learned during his presidential campaign that he had to conserve his strength, to save it for his work as Chief Executive.

He could not rid himself of the feeling that he would be called upon to serve as a "war president." Europe was an armed camp in the spring of 1913, when he became twenty-eighth President, but few Europeans and fewer Americans were aware of war's nearness. Even as he looked ahead and foresaw the tragedy of war, he worked desperately in the little time he had to strengthen foundations in government and business. Because it was his creed that a President should be a leader, an executive with "a certain tough and stubborn fiber," he did not spare himself as head of the nation, and statecraft filled his every moment.

Ellen Wilson, however, found leisure in the White House. She still received callers for her husband, placed papers where he could find them at the moment he wanted, kept herself informed on politics, made his home the quiet haven he needed; but the trained staff of servants relieved her of detail work. In her new-found freedom she had more time for her artistic and philanthropic interests. For years she had been paying for the education of young Southern mountaineers. Now as a member of the Southern Industrial Education Association she interested others in the need for schooling the boys and girls of the Appalachians. Proceeds from the sale of landscapes which she entered in the New York show of the Association of Woman Sculptors and Painters were sent to an industrial school in Rome, Georgia. Membership on the board of the Associated Charities in Washington gave her an active part in social-service work in the capital. She made a survey of housing conditions in the alley tenements and brought congressional attention to the squalor and disease which existed there; so a committee drew up a bill of improvements.

She did little painting, but she made a venture into landscape gardening. At Princeton she had designed the garden for her home there, making a pool surrounded by cedars of Lebanon the central figure, and plotting the ground with tulips and columbine and Canterbury bells for spring, roses for summer, and asters for autumn. At the White House she made a rose garden and lined the President's walk, the path from the Executive Mansion to his offices, with rose trees. She spent many of her days of illness there, watching the gardeners at work from her chair.

So quietly did the presidential family live that few knew of the seriousness of the First Lady's illness. She had not spared herself to better tenement conditions in Washington. Even through the trying times of preparing the White House for two weddings—those of Eleanor Wilson to William Gibbs McAdoo and Jessie Wilson to Francis Sayre— she went on with the work. She had taxed her strength more than any one realized; on August 6, 1914, she died. Just before she became unconscious she whispered to the President that she would be happier if she knew the tenement bill had been passed. Word was sent to Congress, and assurance was returned that legislation would be made.

Her devotion to Woodrow Wilson had protected him while he grew to be a leader of men and nations. She had nurtured the self-faith that was to sustain him in times of trouble. Her work was left in him.

Edith (Bolling) Galt Wilson
(1872–1962)

INTO a drawing room fragrant with flowers came an erect, thin-faced man and a dark-eyed woman dressed in black velvet. A black picture hat accentuated the grace of her head, and the long, pointed sleeve of her afternoon dress reached down the back of her hand, almost hiding the sparkle of the rings she wore; the hand rested on the man's arm. They took their place under a canopy of heather; then began the wedding of Woodrow Wilson, President of the United States, and Edith Bolling Galt.

Like the President, Mrs. Galt—widow of Norman Galt of Washington and daughter of Judge William Holcomb Bolling of Wytheville, Virginia—disliked publicity and pageantry. At her request the wedding was held at her home rather than at the White House. She had spent her married life in Washington but had taken little part in the spectacular social life of the capital. Her charitable work had been done quietly. Society editors found her gracious but uncommunicative. That she was active in social service or that she was a lineal descendant of Pocahontas were both private matters.

When the President and she met at a luncheon in the

White House in 1915 they quickly became friends, and it was not long before he sent her a daily greeting of orchids, her favorite flower. They were married on December 18, 1915. Upon her marriage to the President, Mrs. Wilson began a five-year experience such as no other First Lady had ever lived.

On April 6, 1917, the United States declared war on Germany, and Woodrow Wilson became a "war president." Almost since the beginning of World War I in 1914 there had been pressure upon him to put America into the battle-field; but throughout the days that brought the sinking of the *Lusitania* and the *Sussex* he tried to preserve America's neutrality. As a boy growing up in Augusta, Georgia, he had seen all around him a land that had been devastated by war, a torn and beaten and tired land. In his college days at Princeton and Johns Hopkins he saw in his studies of history and government the harsh rises and tragic dissolutions of warring countries. He knew what war did to nations and their peoples. He would not send his nation into battle so long as he could honorably guard its peace.

When that peace was no longer honorable and when the nation was at last united in its demand for war, he read his war message to Congress.

Then, when he had sent his country to war, he was grim in his determination to win quickly and thoroughly. The man who loved peace more than anything else rose at four-thirty in the morning to get at the work of making war. While he inspired the nation with his idealism and sent thousands to fight not for gain but for justice, the First Lady served with a Washington unit of American Red Cross. Gates to the White House grounds were locked, and behind them worked a man who had the gaunt loneness of

Woodrow Wilson, accompanied by his second wife, Edith

a Lincoln. The First Lady devoted herself to relief work, prepared clothes and bandages for the fighters, helped distracted fathers and mothers who wrote to her rather than to the War Department when their soldier sons were in trouble or missing. Her days were as full as her husband's, but her great task was to come later.

Two months after the signing of the armistice the President and Mrs. Wilson sailed for Europe. Never before had a President gone abroad during his term of his office, nor had a First Lady while she was mistress of the White House. The armistice on November 11, 1918, had ended hostilities; but the President then felt that he must make a fight to ensure lasting and constructive peace; so he broke all precedent and went to Paris for a part in the Peace Conference. At that time he was at the height of his popularity in Europe. People abroad looked upon him as an inspired leader, actually as a savior. With Mrs. Wilson he was entertained at Buckingham Palace in London; in Italy he was given the use of King Victor Emmanuel's royal train, and thousands roared welcome to him at Milan and Turin; Parisian crowds threw bouquets of violets into the presidential carriage as their tribute to the First Lady.

With Lloyd George of England, Clemenceau of France, and Orlando of Italy he effected the Treaty of Versailles; then returned to America to win his country to the League of Nations, his hope of establishing permanent peace throughout the world. He was weakened by influenza, but no one could dissuade him from touring the United States to plead for the League.

Surrounded by secret service men, the President and Mrs. Wilson boarded their special train in Washington for the Western trip. An office force of White House stenographers and clerks and a large group of newspaper reporters accompanied the President on his official journeys. A secret service man preceded the presidential party to inspect stations, routes that the Chief Executive's motor would take through cities where he was to stop, and halls where he was to speak. Ahead of the special train traveled a pilot engine to ensure safety along the tracks.

Though Woodrow Wilson got more rest in his private car than he had enjoyed for several months abroad and at the White House, even that was not enough for him in his weakened condition. On the day after his speech at Pueblo, Colorado, September 26, 1910, he collapsed; and Edith

Bolling Wilson began her work, to carry on for him. At her order the train flashed back to Washington.

At the White House once more, both Admiral Cary T. Grayson, the President's physician, and Mrs. Wilson saw the danger of his illness. She felt, however, that she could not risk unsettling the nation and the world by the grave news. The simple announcement was made that "The President is a very sick man." Then the First Lady became nurse, companion, and executive secretary. The bedridden President could not handle the business of his office alone.

At eight o'clock each morning Mrs. Wilson, dressed in blouse and walking skirt or in a tailored linen dress, joined him for breakfast in his room. After reading the newspapers to him, she read aloud the mail that was essential for him to have. Secretary Tumulty had made the first selection of the letters, and Mrs. Wilson had done the final sorting. As she read them to the President he dictated notes for her to use as the foundation of replies she would write later in the day; then she read to him the summaries she had made of documents and official papers which required his attention.

During his rest period from two until four o'clock in the afternoon she walked or drove. On her return to the White House she received government officials to give them messages from the President, and, over the teacups, to discuss routine business. In the evening she got out memoranda the President had given her, and answered correspondence. To save him effort, she often signed her own name to routine letters, and department heads had praise for the concise and clear notes which came to them bearing the signature of "Edith Bolling Wilson." After caring for the correspondence, she studied documents, pardon pleas and official messages, and made the condensed reviews of them which she would give to the President the following day. Then with the facts before him he could make his decisions. It was far into the night before the executive secretary finished her work.

Outside the locked gates of the White House grounds many were saying that the First Lady was running the country. Others, remembering Woodrow Wilson's invincible belief that a President should be the leader of his country— a belief on which his dynamic idealism was built—questioned that he would, even when unable to leave his bed, surrender that leadership to anyone. At times he had counseled with others, yet never had he been anything but leader.

On his weaker days Mrs. Wilson withheld matters of business from him; when he was stronger she brought them to his attention. Few visitors were admitted to his room, and none were admitted unless Mrs. Wilson accompanied them. As soon as she saw the President tiring she signaled them to leave. When the public heard that she regulated the President's days and was present at all interviews it called her a tyrant. It was a tyranny of mercy.

Through the remainder of his term of office and until his death on February 3, 1924, she served him with a loyalty that even a critical public could but admire. After his death she went abroad annually to visit Geneva, home of the League of Nations—the memorial to the idealism of Woodrow Wilson. In 1931 she accepted the invitation of Poland to attend the unveiling of a statue of him which Ignace Jan Paderewski, statesman and musician, presented to Poland.

Florence (Kling) De Wolfe Harding
(1860–1924)

IF there had been no Florence Kling Harding to spur his ambition, Warren Harding would not have become President of the United States on March 4, 1921.

Even since their marriage in 1891 she had been the one to plan new ventures for him and to rouse him to action. He was gifted with a handsome appearance, a persuasive voice, an orator's sense of the dramatic, an unassuming and artless manner which made friends for him wherever he went. He would have been content to take things as they came; but Mrs. Harding made him put his gifts to work and seek success rather than wait comfortably for what might come along.

Amos Kling, banker of Marion, Ohio, took charge of the training of his daughter Florence from the first day she was able to tumble after him. He had rather hoped that his first child would be a boy; but whatever disappointment he may have felt he concealed by his interest in his daughter. He made a companion of her and trained her as he would have trained a son. He developed in her a sense of self-reliance, a quickness of judgment, an interest in the practical routine of business, and—above all—an energy of mind and spirit.

Throughout her school days and after she returned from the Cincinnati Conservatory of Music to keep house for him and to teach music, and throughout her married life as Florence Kling De Wolfe, her father and she were companions. Then young Warren Harding came to Marion from Caledonia, Ohio, and bought the town's struggling weekly newspaper, the Marion *Star*. He was very likable, but when Florence Kling De Wolfe, then a widow, told her father that she was going to marry Warren Harding, the banker would not give his consent. They were married in 1891, in spite of Amos Kling's protest.

As a weekly the Marion *Star* was making an unobtrusive living for its amiable editor, and he was satisfied. Mrs. Harding was not satisfied. One day she walked briskly down to the office, studied the account books, and decided that the *Star* was not being pushed. It waited for business to come to it. Mrs. Harding changed that passive policy. She took charge of the circulation department of the *Star* and persuaded her husband to change his weekly into a daily paper. Then she went out to make business. For fourteen years she worked as circulation manager, advertising solicitor, reporter and editorial writer, hurrying home each night on her bicycle to cook dinner and do the housework.

As the town grew and the executive energy of Mrs. Harding developed business for the *Star*, the paper prospered. Its editor, Warren Harding, became a leading citizen of Marion. He was active in civic enterprises, banking, and church affairs; he gained influence as an editor and public speaker. Ohio politicians took notice of the genial Warren Harding who made friends so easily and talked so well. They watched his success in local affairs; then sent him to the State Senate and, in 1915, to the United States Senate.

In 1920 they determined to send him to the White
House, but they knew they would have to get Mrs. Harding
to help them keep him in the fight for the presidential
nomination. She went with him to Chicago for the nomi-
nating convention, and it was she who went from the hotel
each morning to the Coliseum and took a place in a box to
study the convention while Warren Harding kept himself
outside the political turmoil.

On the convention floor sat coatless men, irritable under
the strain of listening to speeches as political leaders tried
to break the deadlock. Women delegates unconsciously
pushed hats back from damp foreheads and fanned wanly
against the thick drift of June heat.

In a box sat a poised woman whose calm face was delicately cool looking, whose gray hair was carefully waved and
in perfect order. Her eyes were vigilant. With the skill of a
trained reporter she watched the faces of the delegates
below her—tired faces that she felt would show relief when
Warren Harding's name was presented to break the deadlock. She watched and she waited. At last the convention
nominated Warren Harding.

Back to Marion went the presidential candidate and Mrs.
Harding. From the porch of the green and white house
Warren Harding made his campaign for the presidency,
calling upon America to "return to normalcy." Visitors
found Senator Harding waiting for them. They listened to
his reminiscences of the days when he had taught school,
worked on a railroad, played in a band, set type. They went
back home and voted for him, because he made them his
friends. They voted him into the White House.

Throughout the campaign, the country had warmed to
Senator Harding and his wife, because everything they did

showed them to be "just folks." After eight years of the driving idealism of Woodrow Wilson, America was glad to relax with a President and First Lady who were neighborly people.

Gates to the White House grounds had been closed and locked for almost eight years. The President and Mrs. Harding had them opened at once, making the White House once more the "People's House."

In contrast to Woodrow Wilson, President Harding did not believe that he should lead the nation. All that he wanted to do was to help it. As an editor he had instructed reporters never, if they could avoid it, to write a story for the *Star* that would injure anyone's feelings or reputation. As a politician he had kept himself aloof from quarrels. As a neighbor he had a good word for everyone.

Mrs. Harding, too, reached out a neighborly hand to the public, yet no First Lady observed the formal etiquette of the White House more strictly. Not she but the President demurred when he was served first at the table. It was he who was annoyed when an attendant, barring her way as she moved to step into the elevator, said, "The President enters first, Mrs. Harding." The President frowned. The First Lady smiled and thanked the attendant for the correction.

Although she did not revert to the Roosevelt custom of having three trumpeters herald arrival of the presidential party at receptions, Mrs. Harding entertained with a dignity akin to that of earlier courtly days. Study of the *White House Diary*, a record of the social triumphs and mistakes made by First Ladies, aided her in planning gatherings where people—two thousand or three thousand at a time— could meet the President.

While she conferred with military aides and secretaries, she realized that White House entertainment in the twentieth century was more of a business than a pleasant hour or two of visiting. First she sent engraved cards to three thousand or more guests, then called caterers and White House gardeners into conference.

Not until all of the guests were assembled did the presidential party make its entrance. Military aides in full dress uniform preceded the President and Mrs. Harding down the main stairs. Following them were the Cabinet members and their wives. Saluted by the Marine band, they advanced into the Blue Room where President and First Lady received the guests. No one refused an invitation to the White House. A presidential request is accepted as a social command; more than once a hostess has hurriedly left her own dinner party at the request of the White House to substitute for a guest absent through illness.

Mrs. Harding was acclaimed as one of the most liberal of White House hostesses, yet she found time to be at the President's side whenever he made a public address. She was with him at the dedication of the Lincoln Memorial; with him when, on behalf of the women of America, he presented Madame Marie Curie, co-discoverer of radium, with a gram of the rare element. She was with him at the burial of the Unknown Soldier in Arlington on the third anniversary of the Armistice, November 11, 1921.

Few were aware that the President was finding that government was not a simple thing; but Florence Harding was one who knew. She was powerless to help him, for the very qualities that had taken him to the presidency were

Mrs. Harding receiving delegates from the Filipino Mission

driving him from it. Friends whom he had appointed to office abused his trust in them. Before he realized it, they had despoiled their offices and his honor.

He did not know what to do. Nor did Florence Harding. Together, burdened by their tragic problem, they boarded the presidential train in the summer of 1923 for a tour of Alaska and the Pacific Coast. They thought they would be able to work out some sort of solution before returning to Washington. Somehow, they thought, they would be able to avert the dishonor that faced the Harding administration. They could not. Suddenly the President became ill, and on August 2 in San Francisco he died, with his problem still unsolved. Alone, there was pitifully little that Florence Harding could do to conceal the fact that through him his friends had betrayed public trust. Making one last effort to protect Warren Harding's memory, she destroyed what private papers she could, then quietly went back to Marion. Until her death, a year later, tired and broken by illness. she kept faith in a man whom others had betrayed.

Grace Goodhue Coolidge
(1879–1957)

On the dining-room floor sat a slender, dark-haired woman who was joining lengths of toy train track with the skill that comes from long practice. Deftly she bent a prong here and spread one there. As she fitted curves and switches, two little boys stood close to her, ready to put their engine and cars on the track the moment Mother laid it across the floor for them.

Down went the track; up went the station. Cars were coupled into a train. The engine was wound. Two little boys watched the "Transcontinental Limited" hurtle away on its click-clack course to mountains and cities on the other side of the dining room. While the engineer and conductor squatted on their heels beside the track, the chief-of-construction seated herself in a nearby chair and took up her mending. As she sewed, she looked up whenever the excited engineer or conductor summoned her to ride into the land of make-believe. Her dark eyes brightened, and her wide, sensitive mouth smiled.

As a child, she had enjoyed quiet days in Burlington, Vermont, in woods and fields. Almost without knowing it she set an aim for herself. From her father's friend, Mr.

Yale, she heard of a school in Northampton, Massachusetts, devoted to the teaching of deaf children. Caroline Ardelia Yale, Mr. Yale's sister, was principal of the institute; and as Grace Goodhue learned more and more of the work being done there, she determined to share it. After graduating from the University of Vermont she went to Northampton and for three years taught at the Clarke School for the Deaf.

There was another Vermonter in Northampton. Calvin Coolidge had gone there to study law soon after his graduation from Amherst College. In the autumn of 1905 the two Vermonters were married. For their unassuming home they rented half of a double house at 21 Massasoit Street where two sons, John and Calvin junior, were born. Upon Mrs. Coolidge fell a large part of the training of the boys; during sessions of the Massachusetts state legislature Calvin Coolidge was home only at weekends. His salary as state senator and, later, as lieutenant governor was small. While he worked in Boston, Mrs. Coolidge economically remained at Northampton in the house of her bridal days, sending John and young Calvin to school, sewing for them, working with them, playing with them.

Nor was the way of Calvin and Grace Coolidge changed when Massachusetts elected the quiet man from Northampton to the governorship. The state provided no executive mansion for its governor. Governor Coolidge roomed in Boston and, each Saturday, went home in a day coach to Northampton. Boston knew little of the First Lady of Massachusetts. She was busy being housekeeper and mother.

In summer the family went up to the Vermont hills to stay at Plymouth with Colonel John Coolidge, the governor's father. There the boys helped with farm chores. Mrs.

Coolidge sewed and knitted; and Governor Coolidge, in cowhide boots and a blue woolen smock that had belonged to his grandfather, chopped wood and pitched hay as he had done in his boyhood.

All the strength and simplicity of New England Vermont went into their life, into the training of their sons. They took that strength and simplicity with them when they went to Washington in 1921 as Vice-President of the United States and Second Lady of the Land; but in the two years that Calvin Coolidge quietly devoted himself to the business of being Vice-President, lithe, dark-haired Grace Coolidge emerged from the background. From the placid life of a Northampton housewife she joined the routine of social Washington, and enjoyed herself so much that people enjoyed just being with her.

As they had done before they were national figures, the Vice-President and Mrs. Coolidge went up to Plymouth for their summers. On the night of August 2, 1923, Colonel Coolidge hurriedly climbed the stairs to his son's room to give him the message that President Harding had just died in San Francisco. By the light of a kerosene lamp the father, in his right as a notary public, administered the oath of office by which his son became President of the United States. From the lamp-lighted farmhouse in the Vermont hills the President and First Lady returned to the White House.

Washington had grown since World War I from an amiable, drowsing town of dormer windows and dull red brick. It had become a favorite place for all kinds of conventions, whose members wanted to visit the White House and be photographed with the President or First Lady. They were seldom disappointed, for Mrs. Coolidge posed for hundreds of pictures and shook thousands of hands, all with tireless enthusiasm.

She began her work each day at nine o'clock when, accompanied by her white collie, Prudence Prim, she went up to her "sky parlor," a glass sunroom above the south portico. First she turned on phonograph or radio, then with her secretary sorted the toppling pile of the day's mail into personal letters, invitations, requests to be received at the White House, requests for photographs, for donations to bazaars and benefits, for assistance. After attending to correspondence there was just time for a walk before the reception of visitors began at noon. Enviously a guest once remarked to her, "How wonderful it must be to live here and be able to take a book out under those lovely trees and read."

"I think I have read one book since I came," Mrs. Coolidge replied. She knew what it was to be a public servant, yet she enjoyed it. She found pleasure in being able to share the White House. She took pride in its history and its dignity; but while she was mistress, the Executive Mansion was as much a home as a show place, and young visitors were delighted when a bunchy chow puppy or a piratical raccoon scooted down the hall.

Much as she enjoyed the White House, the ceaseless demands of her position put her under a strain. That was a major reason why Calvin Coolidge refused to be candidate for another term. From his experience in the capital he knew, as he wrote in his autobiography, that "These social functions [in the White House] are almost as much a part of the life of official Washington as a session of Congress or a term of the Supreme Court." He did not want to endanger Mrs. Coolidge's health by letting her assume another

four years of White House responsibility. Telling no one until he summoned reporters one morning, he distributed slips of paper which read, "I do not choose to run in 1928."

Mrs. Coolidge first heard of her husband's decision when a friend came to her three hours later with the greeting, "Quite a surprise the President gave us this morning. Of course you know all about it?" He was astonished by her answer, "I don't believe I do. What was it?"

She, however, was not at all surprised that her husband had neither consulted nor advised her of his decision. Throughout their life together they had seldom discussed his activity in public office. Even when she became First Lady, whatever she learned of the nation's business she learned from newspapers and other common sources. Calvin Coolidge kept his political moves to himself, and Grace Coolidge was satisfied that he was right. Each had his own work. Calvin Coolidge was the public executive and Mrs. Coolidge was mistress of a home, whether it was the one in Northampton or the one in Washington.

No First Lady ever retired from the White House bearing more of the nation's regard than did Grace Coolidge. She entered public life unknown and went out from it the most widely liked woman in all America. From the stately Executive Mansion she returned to Northampton, first to the small plain house at 21 Massasoit Street, then to the newly purchased estate, The Beeches, resuming private life with the spirit that had delighted two little boys long before it had charmed a nation.

Lou Henry Hoover

(1875–1944)

BEHIND bags of rice and sugar, desperately stacked into a barricade, the defenders of Tientsin husbanded their ammunition and grimly wondered how long they could hold the city. Before them raged the fanatical Boxer horde. "Death to Foreigners!" cried that remnant of Old China in its determination to exterminate European and American residents. "Death to Foreigners!" was the battle cry of the thousands of Boxers who stormed Tientsin and shelled the beleaguered Foreign Concession.

Food was scarce in the barricaded Concession; water scant. Shells burst in the streets. Bullets smashed into walls and ricocheted.

With as little apparent concern as though she were pedaling along the campus of Leland Stanford University, Lou Henry Hoover cycled to her post at the hospital. Sharp bursts from five-inch guns manned by the Boxers and the whine of bullets sounded very different from the clean crack of the rifle with which she had hunted back home in California. The Boxer gunfire was war fire; but she had work to do. She kept on her way to the hospital.

When the Boxers had turned on Tientsin she had wasted

no time thinking of danger. At once she went to the temporary hospital and learned first-aid work. Soon she was doing even more than caring for the wounded under fire. The little nursing station was ill equipped to serve the scores of wounded who were carried to it from behind the barricade each day; so Mrs. Hoover made determined bicycle raids from one end of the Concession to the other, getting material for dressings and bandages.

Not for three weeks did relief come to the defenders of Tientsin, not until American, European, and Japanese troops fought their way into China and marched into shell-shattered Tientsin. Roads were then opened to foreigners for escape; but the Hoovers did not leave. Herbert Hoover, who had directed construction of a defense for the town, gave his engineering services to the American troops; and, at the request of army surgeons, Mrs. Hoover stayed on to work at the hospital. The hospital staff had learned what others were to learn as she worked with them, that a task seemed easier somehow when Mrs. Hoover was there.

In the year and a half since her marriage, life had moved rapidly for her. At eleven o'clock one morning in February of 1899 she had been married at her home in Monterey, California, to Herbert Clark Hoover. At eleven-forty-seven the same morning they boarded a train for San Francisco; a few hours later they sailed for China where Mr. Hoover was to begin his work as director of mines for the government.

To the surprise of the foreign colonies in Tientsin and Peking, Mrs. Hoover accompanied her husband whenever she could on his trips into the interior of China. Throughout her girlhood in California she had gone up into the hills on camping trips with her father. Sometimes she hiked fifteen or twenty miles, learning that free, tireless stride which marked her as one who was at home in the open. Often she had saddled Pinto or Buckskin and ridden back into the mountains above Monterey. Sometimes she had hunted small game to get specimens for her hobby of taxidermy.

When winter weather made further exploration of the Chinese interior impractical, Herbert Hoover compiled a report of his summer's work. Mrs. Hoover helped him write it. When she had gone up to Palo Alto in 1894 to enter Leland Stanford University she had determined to major in geology. One day while she was in the laboratory, Professor Brannin, her instructor, pointed to some specimens, saying, "Hoover brought them in from the field. They have been called carboniferous; but I think they are pre-carboniferous. Isn't that your opinion, Hoover?" Lou Henry, the freshman, looked up and saw a tall, slender senior, Herbert Hoover, standing beside her.

That was the introduction she had to the mining engineer she was to marry after she had completed her university work. Not long after she had received her B.A. degree—the first woman to be graduated from Stanford with a major in geology—she got a cablegram from Herbert Hoover, who was working in the Australian bush. She cabled back her answer, "Yes," and prepared for her wedding and the journey out to the Orient.

From the time she made that first trip with her husband, she went on almost all of the jaunts that took him, from 1900 to 1914, to Ceylon and Siberia, Australia and Egypt, Europe, and Japan—here, there, and everywhere. Wherever they went, she made a home for him. No matter how short their stay, she at once rented a house.

Of all the temporary homes made by Mrs. Hoover the favorite perhaps was the Red House in London. There in the city which was the world center of mining affairs they took an old house near Kensington Gardens, lined the walls with their books, installed the treasures they had picked up on their travels, and housed their sons' pets—Rags the dog; cages of Japanese seed birds, green parrakeets; Persian and Siamese cats. Behind the long brick wall of the house they made their own garden, for their hobby was still the out-of-doors.

They were living in San Francisco in 1914 when the Panama Exposition commissioned Herbert Hoover to arrange with European countries to send exhibits to the fair. At the end of her sons' school term Mrs. Hoover sailed for Europe and joined her husband in London. They were summering there at the Savoy Hotel at the beginning of World War I. Hundreds of Americans fled from the Continent to London and were stranded in the city without means of getting back to the United States. By official request Herbert Hoover took charge of returning the refugees to America, and Mrs. Hoover once again put her executive ability to work. She organized a committee to help the American women, many of whom were caught without funds by the emergency. In the ballroom and corridors of the Savoy Hotel the Hoover relief corps reassembled families that had been separated in the escape from Europe, cashed checks and advanced traveling money for people they had never before seen, got them passage on the few available steamers for America.

They had scarcely finished that work when Mr. Hoover was asked to direct food administration for Belgium. The outbreak of war had disrupted his fortune; if he were to rebuild it he would have to devote his entire time to business. The decision that he made was to give up business and serve, paying all of his own expenses, as chairman of the Commission for Relief in Belgium. He did not leave his post as head of the relief work until he returned to America to become food administrator, when he taught his own country how to "Hooverize" in wartime.

During the greater part of those war years Mrs. Hoover stayed in California; there they built their home when Mr. Hoover returned to rest and be with his family—"really a very nice family, you know," was what his wife had assured him as he prepared to join her and the boys. At least they could have the home they wanted—not just a temporary home, but one they were going to build for themselves just where they wanted it, and that was to be on the campus of the university where they had gone to school.

Mrs. Hoover took charge of the design. Her husband watched her work away on her plans. First of all, the architects learned, Mrs. Hoover's house must be built so it would take in as much as possible of the out-of-doors. A house, she agreed, must have walls and a roof; but her house was also going to have sky, grass, flowers, trees. It did have.

On the crest of San Juan hill in Palo Alto rose a white stucco building in which the arrangement of terraces and roof space was similar to that of Algerian houses. There was even an outside fireplace on the main terrace so that the family could use the outdoor living room in all weather. Flowers and shrubs there were planted in Japanese oil tubs, the staves bound by bamboo. Tall cypress trees and vines grew within the garden walls. An outdoor swimming pool caught glints of sunlight.

For a year, nothing took the travelers from their home.

The Hoovers with their two sons and daughter-in-law

They talked and read on the terrace. They rode up into the Sierras to camp beside hard-running, cold mountain streams where they cooked over fires built Indian-fashion from chips and twigs; where they set out their bed rolls and scooped hollows in the ground for their shoulders and hips, then eased down into their blankets and slept beneath starry mountain skies.

In 1921, Mr. Hoover was appointed Secretary of Commerce in President Harding's cabinet and reappointed to that post by President Coolidge. For the major part of those eight years "home" was a house on S Street in Washington. As a cabinet lady, Mrs. Hoover not only took her place as an official hostess in the capital but led in the national Girl Scout movement. She was as active in councils and at rallies as she was in camp, when she directed classes, led in story-telling round the fire at night, and turned out before breakfast for bird walks. Goucher College formally recognized her leadership when it awarded her in 1931 an honorary LL.D. degree for activity in social service, particularly that in interest of Girl Scouts.

To her friends Mrs. Hoover often said that her own particular work was to provide a background for her husband. Those who knew her best realized that she did much more than provide a background. Besides taking part in many social welfare movements, she was constantly contriving ways in which to help her husband. Not that she could do his work, but she could and did take over many details so that he might devote himself to his projects. Particularly after he became President in 1929 was she able to spare him from demands on his time and strength, often substituting for him at public ceremonies. Until then she had avoided public appearances and had even refused to grant interviews; but as First Lady, to relieve Mr. Hoover of the burden, she received delegations and addressed assemblies. She made trips to appear at college commencements, to christen a giant dirigible, to send merchant ships down the ways into the sea.

Many women helped their husbands all along the way to the presidency; then, once in the White House, bowed to tradition and limited themselves to performing social duties. Others, like Sarah Polk and Abigail Fillmore, continued as First Ladies to work with their husbands, but remained in the background as unknown counselors, very much like "silent partners."

Just as the country had grown, however, so had the public's demands upon the President. As improved methods of transportation joined the coasts and borders of America, a President was more and more called upon to leave Washington and visit cities, speak at dedications and at openings of public works. A President, if he were to give proper attention to his administrative work, could not accept all the invitations that merited his acceptance. Nor could he accept them and allow just any distinguished person to substitute for him. His substitute had to be someone who would symbolize his honored position.

That problem was solved when Lou Henry Hoover became First Lady. Tradition stood in her way, but she met the challenge, went about her new work of making addresses, receiving honorary degrees, and sending vessels down the ways into the sea.

Eleanor Roosevelt
(1884–1963)

A LONG-LEGGED little girl stood in the doorway of her mother's room. It was teatime, when a winter day is friendliest. In the tall, narrow brownstone house the gaslight was being turned on, and its glow touched and softened the heavy furniture. That was the hour when it seemed good to be inside, to be in your own home—where you belonged.

But the eyes of the child standing in the doorway were clouded. The full, drooping mouth found it hard to smile. For there was a visitor in the room, and the child knew what to expect. Awkwardly she stood there, wishing that she could go; but her mother called gently, and she stepped forward, stiffly, solemnly.

Mrs. Roosevelt turned to the visitor, saying, "This is my daughter Eleanor." And she added gaily, with no thought of wounding, "She's such a funny child—so old-fashioned that we always call her Granny."

"Such a funny child." Eleanor Roosevelt had heard it so often. And each time it hurt just as much. She knew that she did not "belong." She was the "ugly duckling"—a dreamy, shy, awkward child born into a family distinguished for its charm and social leadership. Her mother was the beautiful Anna Hall. Her father was Elliott Roosevelt, younger brother of Theodore who was later to become twenty-fifth President of the United States. The Roosevelts —the name, in Dutch, means "field of roses"—were active patriots during the American Revolution. Down through the years the Roosevelts and the Halls held high rank in the aristocracy of New York City.

Into this background of means and social grace Anna Eleanor Roosevelt was born, in New York City, on October 11, 1884, the first of three children. She was handicapped from the first by her lack of beauty. As she grew, she became lanky and stiff-moving. To overcome a spinal curvature, she wore a brace on her back for years.

In a family accustomed to beauty and to poise, this lack of light, pleasant graces set Eleanor aside. No one meant to hurt or to tease her, but, without being told, she knew that somehow she was "left out."

To try to make up for Eleanor's unattractive appearance, Mrs. Roosevelt spent patient hours to perfect her manners and to develop her mind and character. She read aloud to her daughter, coached her speech, and trained her to memorize poems and Bible verses. But these efforts only sharpened Eleanor's realization of her handicap. Only with her father did she feel at home. He understood her and shared with her his love of music and song. And, most of all, his pride in her gave a little of the confidence she needed so badly. But his health became undermined, and he was with her seldom. Loneliness drove Eleanor into a small world of her own, where she most enjoyed thinking of her father and playing by herself—in a housemaid's sewing room, with cookies and cambric tea for a feast.

But it was not a selfish, sulking loneliness in which she

forgot all about other people. Even as a very little child it hurt her to have others hurt. In Italy, when she was only five and a half, her father had hired a donkey for her and a donkey boy to go with her on rides over the white stone roads. But when the stones cut the boy's bare feet, Eleanor climbed down from the saddle and made him ride while she walked the rest of the way.

From Italy the Roosevelts went to France, where Eleanor was sent to school in a convent. She knew not a word of French, nor was she a Catholic. Again she was an outsider. Hungering for affection, she played a trick to get attention. She told a nun that she had swallowed a penny. Now, she thought, everyone would take an interest in her. But the truth was clear. Her mother took her home, scolding her severely, unable to understand that her daughter would lie.

Nor did Eleanor herself understand it until years later. As a child, she only knew that rather than face a scolding she would tell a falsehood to escape it. If a mere spanking were certain—quick, physical punishment—she told the truth. But, starved for tenderness and aware of her short-comings, she could not bear more criticism or reproach. Not until she realized that everyone has some faults did she overcome fear of criticism, and so overcome the fear that drove her to lie. As she wrote, when a woman, "My mother did not understand that a child may lie from fear; I myself never understood it until I reached the age when I suddenly realized that there was nothing to fear."

In the winter of 1892, when Eleanor was eight, her mother died. Life in another house began for Eleanor and her two small brothers. They went to stay with Grand-mother Hall, with their aunts Pussie and Maude and their uncles Eddie and Vallie. Eleanor's father was seldom able to visit them, but she still wove her dreams around him until his death in August, 1894. In winter the Halls and the children lived in New York; the summers were spent at Oak Terrace, a large lamplit old home at Tivoli on the Hudson River. For the first time Eleanor had something like real companionship. Pussie, Maude, Eddie and Vallie, though years older than she, played with her, took her on walks and drives and read and sang with her.

But all her time could not be spent in their company. She had lessons to do, including French, music, and—because Grandmother Hall worried that her tall Eleanor would need balance and grace—hours of ballet practice. She had almost no friends of her own age. She could not learn how to make them in a life kept so sheltered and secluded. Grandmother Hall believed that the best way to develop Eleanor's character was to discipline her firmly. Nor was the child ever able to escape supervision, for, like all girls in New York society of that day, she was accompanied everywhere by her maid.

Meeting young people her own age only showed how ill prepared she was for their skill in sports, their grace in dancing, their lighthearted fun with one another. Once or twice Grandmother Hall permitted Eleanor and her brother Hall to visit the Theodore Roosevelt family at Sagamore Hill on Oyster Bay. There Eleanor's favorite companion was not one of her cousins, who so easily outdistanced her at sports and games, but her "Uncle Ted." Each Christmas brought something of an ordeal, for she had to attend the annual family party given by Theodore's sister, Aunt Corinne, who did her best to make the child enjoy herself. But there is little pleasure when your clothes are plain and awkward, when you are so shy you would rather sit than dance, and when girls your age tell you about your short-comings "for your own good." And it is hard to be at ease with boys when you see them only once a year. It is even harder to sit with the chaperones and have them arrange dances for you after nearly everyone else has a partner. No wonder Eleanor gratefully remembered, for years, the time when Franklin Delano Roosevelt, a fifth cousin, came up to her and asked her permission to be her partner.

Red-letter days were the friendly times she spent with Victor, the butler, learning to wash and dry dishes, and the steamy, sudsy hours in the laundry at Tivoli with cheerful Mrs. Overhalse, the laundress. When the Halls vacationed at Bar Harbor, Eleanor's chief companion was the elderly hotel owner, with whom she went fishing and climbed the wet, jagged rocks of the Maine coast.

But best of all were the times when Pussie or Vallie or someone else in the family sent her on errands or asked her help in some little chore. One night when Pussie was ill with a sore throat, she asked Eleanor to bring some ice. The icebox was kept in the back yard—down three flights of dark stairs, through the blackness of the basement, and out into the night. The thought of it terrified Eleanor; but she went, for nothing else was so important to the lonely child as was helping someone.

When she was fifteen, she was sent to school in England. New days opened for her. Grandmother Hall did not let Eleanor know that she had asked the headmistress to help the girl correct her many social handicaps. Eleanor had the advantage of believing that she was on her own. At last she had the chance to think for herself, to find out what things she could do.

At Allenswood, the English girls' school, her first task was to fit herself into a group of girls of her own age. She began by taking up a team sport, field hockey, and worked at it until she made the team. It was perhaps the first triumph in all her life, not because she was proud of her skill, but because for the first time she had the warm feeling of "belonging"—at last she had earned a place for herself.

In later years she looked back on the time when she had made the team, and wrote, "I think that day was one of the proudest moments of my life."

Eleanor was fortunate in the choice of Allenswood; for the headmistress was Mlle Souvestre, a white-haired Frenchwoman who had come to England after the terrors of the Franco-Prussian War. The aim of this alert, independent teacher was to spur the girls into thinking for themselves. Well-traveled and cultured, she enriched their backgrounds with her own experience and broadened their standards of judgment by showing them that their own little lives were only parts of a large and closely joined world. She, more than anyone else, helped Eleanor in those younger years to lay the groundwork for the independence, the tolerance, and the active interest in humanity which were later to make Eleanor Roosevelt a leader in America.

From the white-haired woman who had lived so long and so well, Eleanor learned that nearly everything was interesting if she opened her eyes to see it. As her interests and activities widened, there were less time and room in which to think of herself; and so confidence began to grow. Each year at Allenswood with Mlle Souvestre made Eleanor a little more sure of herself. The tall, slender young girl seemed to have found her place at last.

But New York changed it all again. In keeping with family tradition, Grandmother Hall wanted Eleanor to make her debut into society at eighteen. And so the girl came home from England to step back into a world ruled by charm and beauty. All her shyness returned. Every party, every dinner, was a struggle for her. Little by little, however, she made a few close friends. Among them was Franklin Roosevelt, who was in his senior year at Harvard. In the autumn of 1903, when Eleanor was nineteen, they became engaged, and a year later the announcement was made.

Their wedding day was March 17, 1905. They had little choice in the date, for they had to select a day that would fit in with the busy program of the President of the United States, Theodore Roosevelt—"Uncle Ted"—who was to give the bride away. And his schedule called for him to be in New York on March 17 to review the St. Patrick's Day parade. The streets around the house were thickly guarded by police and secret service men to protect the President. Several wedding guests had such difficulty getting through the guard lines that they arrived after the ceremony.

At the end of the school year at Columbia, where Franklin Roosevelt was studying law, they went abroad on their honeymoon. While visiting Scotland, Eleanor was invited to open a bazaar; but she asked her husband to make the speech because, as she said later, "I was quite certain that I could never utter a word aloud in a public place."

The first years of married life were not easy. Eleanor Roosevelt knew nothing about cooking, rearing children, or managing a household. She was almost entirely dependent upon her mother-in-law and her servants. She was still unsure of herself, but she also had extremely strict standards of conduct and did not yet know how to make allowance for small failings in other people.

But her own strong character and the ability which Mlle Souvestre had helped her to build were not gone. When, in 1910, Eleanor Roosevelt came to the turning point of her life, she had the resources to meet it. In that year she began her long career in public life. Her husband was elected to the Senate of the State of New York, and the family moved to Albany for sessions of the legislature. As in England, Eleanor was again on her own—in new surroundings, with new people, with new tasks, and with decisions largely up to her. And again she measured up to the responsibility. She arranged the family life so that her home could be a meeting place for Franklin Roosevelt's political associates and so took her first lessons in politics.

The three years in Albany prepared her well for public life in Washington, which she entered in 1913 when Franklin Roosevelt became Assistant Secretary of the Navy in the administration of President Wilson. She knew the endless demands made upon "official wives," and dutifully spent day after day calling at the homes of official Washington.

When war struck in 1917, Eleanor Roosevelt grew into a leader. The need to organize her household to free herself for war work forced her to develop an executive ability. She continued to entertain officially; supervised her five children; managed a household shaken by the late hours of many emergency meetings in the Navy Department; and yet spent most of her waking hours in Red Cross work, with several days a week given to cooking and serving in a canteen in the railroad yards. Though still miserably shy, she fought shyness down when she saw need for action: noticing that a naval hospital unit for shell-shocked patients was poorly equipped, she made a report directly to the Secretary of the Interior.

She was still little more than an onlooker in political affairs when her husband was nominated in 1920 as Democratic candidate for Vice-President. But the four-week campaign tour that she made with him west to the Rockies added greatly to her political education. She learned how to stand up for public inspection, appear on railroad platforms, face impatient audiences in auditoriums, greet crowds cheerfully at almost any time of the day or night. Once aloof from "the curiosity of the press," she found that the newspapermen who accompanied them on the train were thoughtful, generous, and often helpful. Through them she learned to see the humorous side of many difficulties, and her patience and her tolerance grew. From her husband's chief assistant, Louis McHenry Howe of Albany, she learned to take a critical interest in political issues.

After the election, in which the Democrats were defeated, Eleanor Roosevelt joined the state board of the League of Women Voters. Her duty was to make monthly reports on national legislation, which meant study of long and wordy bills brought before Congress. But in the summer of 1921 all her outside interests came to an end. Franklin Roosevelt was stricken with infantile paralysis. Every moment was given to helping him.

Within a few months, however, this led her back into politics. Her husband's recovery greatly depended upon reawakening his interest in outside affairs, so Eleanor Roosevelt took up political work in order to bring public affairs closely home to her husband. Painfully but determinedly, she learned to make speeches, gratefully receiving every pointer given by the patient Louis Howe. He was gentle but honest with her, and from him she learned to curb her nervous laugh and to prepare her speeches adequately.

Eleanor Roosevelt was growing in other ways too. With her husband crippled and unable to share in the active life

of the children, she undertook to fill his place. From childhood she had been something of a physical coward, afraid
of heights, speed, and water. To prepare herself, she went
to the Y.W.C.A. and learned to swim long after the age
most people begin. Although she hated automobiles, she
learned to drive. And they went on a camping trip, driving
through Quebec and on to their summer home on Campo-
bello Island in New Brunswick. While on that trip, camping out in tents in any pleasant spot, she discovered the
pleasure of striking up chance acquaintanceships, and she
never lost it. She became interested in people of all ages, in
all kinds of work.

When Franklin Roosevelt became Governor of New
York state in 1928, Eleanor was well launched on her dual
career of public work and of helping her husband. On their
farm near Hyde Park she established the Val Kill furniture
factory to give employment to men of the neighborhood. In
New York she bought part interest in the Todhunter School
for Girls, became vice principal, and taught classes in civics.
She managed the executive mansion in Albany, continued
her political work, and took part in state welfare programs.

Her four summers in Albany excellently trained her for
work she was to do later in investigating national social conditions. It was on the summer trips with Governor Roosevelt that she visited all state institutions in New York. Since
Governor Roosevelt could not walk easily he appointed her
to be his unofficial investigator, teaching her to scrutinize
even the smallest details of equipment, hospital care, recreation facilities, cleanliness, and food preparation. Wherever
she went, little escaped her.

Never before had the wife of a President taken such public part in the life of the nation as Eleanor Roosevelt did

Summer, 1941: The Roosevelts relax at their Hyde Park home.

when she became First Lady in 1933. The distress of unemployment uncovered needs too sharp and too wide to be ignored. People were hungry; thousands lived in houses scarcely fit for animals; tens of thousands were without hope.

Seeing the need, Eleanor Roosevelt plunged in to meet it. She was censured for "going back on her word" that she would stay out of national affairs. But those who knew her remembered her sensible explanation, "As they think it over and keep on learning, they may change their minds, just as I have changed mine many times."

To bring the President first-hand information on conditions throughout the nation, she traveled from one end of the country to the other. In one year, by train and airplane and automobile, she journeyed more than forty-three thousand miles.

Eleanor knew that her work was helping Franklin Roosevelt in his task as President. Not only was it difficult for him to get around, but also he was overburdened by the work put on him by the business depression. From all sides came people with suggestions, with criticisms, with demands that the government try one experiment after another. There were few advisers to whom he could turn with confidence. One whom he trusted completely, from experience, was Eleanor Roosevelt.

There was almost no part of the nation which she did not touch. There was almost no field of social service which she did not investigate. Year after year she kept up the record-breaking pace. In addition to her travels she wrote a daily newspaper column called "My Day," spoke on the radio, and made lecture tours—giving her earnings largely to charities. Working while traveling, even dictating to her secretary as they stopped their automobile for a few minutes of picnic lunch, she wrote her autobiography. It was called *This Is My Story* and was one of the most honest and encouraging life stories ever written. When at home in the White House she held regular press conferences with women reporters, the first press meetings ever held by the wife of a President.

Nor did she shirk official entertainment. In one year she presided at teas for 22,353 people; at receptions she shook hands with 16,650 guests; she entertained 319 house guests and had 485 guests at various meals. That same year she attended to about 10,000 letters on personal matters and supervised the handling of more than 74,000 communica-

Mrs. Roosevelt meeting with a UN group at Hyde Park

tions on routine or official affairs. Yet she always found
time to entertain government officials, guests, and visitors
from foreign lands at informal picnics at Hyde Park, where
she helped to cook and serve the outdoor meals.

In 1945, Eleanor Roosevelt began her thirteenth consecutive year as First Lady—a record no one is likely to match,
since legislation now limits a President to two terms. For
Eleanor and Franklin Roosevelt, those thirteen years had
been times of trouble in the White House, from the depression days of the '30's through the violence of World
War II. And the war was still raging in March 1945,
when President Roosevelt went to Warm Springs, Georgia,
for a short rest. For a man already weakened by polio, the
demanding years as Chief Executive proved too great, and
he died on April 12. The nation, saddened by the news,
felt it a double tragedy that he had not lived to see the final
victory of World War II, through which he had so ably
led his country.

Eleanor did not retire from her public-spirited work; she
exerted herself for the United Nations, in hopes of pre-
venting another such war. She was a delegate to its first
General Assembly, Chairman of the Commission on Human Rights, and she had a major part in shaping the
Universal Declaration of Human Rights. At the time of her
death in 1963, she was working on a plan to raise money
for the Wiltwyck School for Boys. She had come a long
way from the shy, ungainly, moody little girl of 1890. Year
by year, she had overcome one handicap after another,
learning each lesson hard, but learning it.

Bess Wallace Truman

(1885)

It was four o'clock in the morning, March 1918. Chill winds swept Independence, Missouri. Suddenly the telephone in the large white frame house at 219 North Delaware Street began to ring—and rang—and rang. Lights suddenly shone through the brightly colored, leaded windows as a startled young woman—Bess Wallace—rushed sleepily to the phone.

At the sound of the voice coming over long-distance, she became fully awake. The caller was Lieutenant Harry S Truman, to whom she was engaged. He had just gotten off a troop train at Kansas City, Kansas, the first leg of his journey to combat duty in France during World War I.

He later described that predawn call with a smile, saying: "I . . . asked a railroad switchman if I could call my fiancée in Independence, and he said, 'Call her, the phone's yours, but if she doesn't break the engagement at four o'clock in the morning, she really loves you.'"

Bess Wallace was devoted to Harry Truman, whom she had known since their childhood in Independence. They had gone through school together, and had spent their time together whenever possible in the years after graduation.

Harry Truman has often said, "There was never any other girl for me. I've loved Bess since the first time I saw her." That first time was when Bess Wallace was a very little girl in Sunday school.

Bess was born in Independence on February 13, 1885. She was christened Elizabeth Virginia Wallace, but was always called Bess.

When Bess was five years old a family moved from nearby Grandview to Independence—it was the Truman family, and Harry Truman was six. Harry's parents—John and Martha Ellen Truman—moved from their farm at Grandview so their children could have the advantage of town schooling. They settled in a pleasant home that John Truman, a livestock dealer, bought on Chrysler Street. At the rear were quarters for the Truman cook, her husband the gardener, and their family.

Mrs. Truman immediately enrolled Harry in Sunday school, where he first saw Bess. After he became President of the United States, he told an interviewer: "When I was about six years old, my mother took me to Sunday school and I saw there the prettiest, sweetest little girl I'd ever seen. She had golden curls and blue eyes. I was too backward even to look at her very much, and I didn't speak to her for years."

After he mustered his courage and spoke to her, he became her shadow. "From the fifth grade until our graduation from high school we were in the same classes," he said later. "If I succeeded in carrying her books to school or back home for her I had a big day."

Bess excelled in tennis, she ice-skated and roller-skated gracefully and daringly, and she rode well. Sometimes she went fishing with her three younger brothers, and calmly

baited her own hook. The neighborhood boys admired her
baseball skill.

Many times, after school hours, Bess and Harry and their
classmates gathered to plan school activities. There were
forty-one in that class of 1901—thirty girls and eleven boys.
The girls looked old for their years—like young matrons—
in their high-necked shirtwaists and long full skirts. They
wore their hair long and puffed—there were no permanents
in 1901, just kid curlers. The boys in the class also seemed
older, like respectable young bank clerks. They all wore
neat, short, tight-buttoned jackets, long narrow trousers,
white shirts, high stiff collars with ties carefully knotted up
under the chin, and sometimes a gold watch chain looped
across the chest.

On warm moonlit nights they went on hay rides, and
there were summer picnics in wooded Idlewild. In winter
they sang on bobsled parties, or skated on Bryant's Pond
till time to troop into someone's warm kitchen for cookies
and hot chocolate.

After graduating from Independence High, Bess commuted to Kansas City, Missouri, to attend the Barstow
School for Girls.

In 1903 the Trumans lost their property. They moved to
Kansas City, where Harry and his brother worked as bank
clerks. For the next three years he commuted as often as he
could to visit Bess in Independence. No girl in town had
more dates than Bess, but she always managed to find time
for Harry Truman.

The trips were a little harder to make when Harry was
called to Grandview to work his Grandmother Young's
six-hundred-acre farm. But not even Missouri mudholes
made the difficult journey to Independence and Bess.

He managed the big farm so successfully that in 1913 he bought an automobile. There were few cars in Missouri, so he made quite an impression as he chugged up Delaware Street to take Bess for a ride.

Then came the tumultuous years of World War I. Harry was made a second lieutenant in the National Guard field artillery. He and Bess became engaged in 1918, before he left for France.

In May of 1919 he was mustered out as a major, and hurried back to Bess in Missouri. On June 28 they were married in the little red brick Trinity Episcopal Church in Independence.

Bess wore a simple white dress. Instead of a veil, a wide, graceful garden hat covered her blond hair. She carried a prayer book, rather than a bouquet.

After their honeymoon in Chicago and Detroit, Bess and Harry settled in the Wallace home at 219 North Delaware.

For the next two years they lived comfortably. Harry and Edward Jacobson, who had served as sergeant under his command, established a men's furnishing store in Kansas City. Then early in 1922 a severe business depression swept the Midwest. The firm of Truman and Jacobson failed.

Edward Jacobson declared bankruptcy; but Harry Truman wanted to pay his own debts. That would mean making a new start and then cutting living expenses to the bone. He talked it over with Bess. It was the first hard decision for them, but they made it together, and they chose to pay.

It took some fifteen years to clear the debt, but they did it. In those long years Bess learned to weigh every penny. She had grown up in comparative wealth, yet she didn't complain. Instead, she studied every possibility that would help them save to make payments. She formed habits of thrift that she carried with her into the White House.

The day of February 17, 1924 brought Harry and Bess great happiness—that was the day their daughter, (and only child) was born. They christened her Mary Margaret, which soon became just Margaret. The little girl was blue-eyed and golden-haired like her mother.

Harry Truman was enormously proud of his wife and daughter, and they would do anything for him. He tended to spoil Margaret as a child, but thoroughly agreed with Bess's insistence that the little girl learn good manners and proper language. The one time he really laid down the law to her was when she persisted in using slang. He fined her ten cents for every offense. She soon stopped.

In 1934, when Margaret was ten years old, Harry Truman was elected United States senator from Missouri. Still striving to pay off that business debt, they took only a small apartment on Connecticut Avenue in Washington, D.C. Bess did her own housework.

Harry Truman discussed with Bess every important issue of his work as senator. She even worked in his office for a time as an unpaid clerk. As his activities in Congress grew, she joined his staff as a full-time salaried worker. He declared, "I don't know where I'd get a more efficient or willing worker." After he became President of the United States, he credited her thinking and judgment with much of his success in political life. Bess herself once said, with wry humor, "I've been in politics over twenty-five years."

He was re-elected senator in 1940. Bess and Margaret almost regretted his election victory. They longed for the day when they could return to private life in Independence.

That time was long in coming. In 1944, people were sure

that Franklin D. Roosevelt would be nominated for a fourth term by the Democratic party. The only question was—who would be nominated as Vice-President? The Democratic convention was held in August in Chicago. Harry Truman drove Bess and Margaret to Chicago, then prepared to take a routine part in the convention.

But it turned out to be far from routine. President Roosevelt sent word that he wanted Harry Truman to be his Vice-President.

Through the next day of nominations and balloting, Bess sat in a box in the convention hall, dreading the moment when the delegates would swing to Harry Truman. That evening, under the hot lights of the steel-girded convention hall, the roll call droned on until suddenly one state after another shouted its votes for "Harry S Truman!" Then cameramen, reporters, and broadcasters swarmed up to Harry Truman on the platform and Bess Truman, sitting silent and grave in her box. Homey Independence seemed very far away.

Remembering that night, Harry Truman later said: "After my nomination and return to the hotel with police and secret service men, none of us was very happy." Bess is reported to have murmured, as their car roared through the crowds to the hotel, "Are we going to have to go through this all the rest of our lives?"

Bess and Harry Truman realized they were facing a graver situation than usually confronted a nominee for the Vice-Presidency. They, among many people in Washington, felt that President Roosevelt's health was failing after the long strain of the war years. If he should be re-elected and then die before finishing his fourth term in office, the burden of the Presidency would fall on Harry Truman.

After the inauguration in January 1945, the Trumans were swept into the social life expected of a Vice-President and his family. Bess, reared in the Southern traditions of Independence, competently went about her role. Both she and Harry Truman insisted that Margaret be kept from public life as much as possible, yet protocol demanded she attend some functions. The gay and popular Margaret began to enjoy dinners and receptions; but she was attending George Washington University, too, where she was majoring in history and international relations. She also spent hours studying voice.

The Trumans had less than three months to adjust to their new obligations. Late in March 1945 President Roosevelt went to Warm Springs, Georgia, for a brief rest. In Washington, Harry Truman methodically went about his job as Vice-President. On April 12 he walked from his office to consult with the Speaker of the House of Representatives. He got there at 5:05 P.M. The phone rang almost at once. It was a call from the White House, asking him to come there immediately.

Mrs. Roosevelt was waiting for him in her study on the second floor. As he entered, she told him that President Roosevelt had died at 3:35 that afternoon in Warm Springs.

He telephoned Bess and, in a voice strained by shock and worry, notified her and sent a car to their Connecticut Avenue apartment to bring his family to the White House. He took the oath of office at 7:08 that evening. At 7:09 Harry Truman was President of the United States, and Bess Truman was the First Lady of the Land.

The colorful, spectacular days of the Roosevelt family in the White House were over. Though the reluctant Truman family had not sought their new life, each member—Harry, Bess, and Margaret—at once set out to do their best in unwelcome jobs. Bess Truman determinedly kept out of the press as much as possible. She discontinued the news conferences started by Mrs. Franklin D. Roosevelt, and made no attempt to have any open part in political life.

Fully aware, however, of the demands on her as First Lady, Bess greeted hundreds of visiting groups, christened ships and planes, opened bazaars, attended banquets, gave state dinners, and shook so many hands a day that sometimes she had to rest her own right hand in a whirlpool bath. Her dignity and reserve in public seemed almost formidable. It was difficult for her to meet strangers. She had no gift for the easy small talk so important in being hostess to the public. Bess Truman could readily discuss any subject of major importance, and she preferred serious, considered conversation. Yet, with friends she knew well, she was a lively, warmhearted companion.

The public grew to admire her. Her dignity and integrity commanded respect. In her early days in the White House she gave little thought to style in dressing. For most of her life, far more important things than clothes had occupied her. But, though she never liked being First Lady and even disliked the title, she assumed the obligation of the position. She knew that the public wanted a First Lady to dress smartly, so Bess Truman quietly went to a leading dressmaker for her wardrobe. She bought carefully and well, never extravagantly, with an eye to unobtrusive long wear and possible remodeling.

Margaret undertook her role easily. Like her father, she was pleasantly at home with people in any group, small or great. Her quick smile was a friendly greeting for everyone. She got her lively sense of humor from both her father and

Mrs. Truman saw Margaret off on a trip to Europe.

mother; and her wit and her grace as a dancer made her one of the most popular girls in Washington.

But Margaret had more in mind than a social career. She wanted a career as a singer. When she asked her parents' permission, Bess and Harry Truman requested that she finish college first. Margaret respected their wish with her usual good grace. When she graduated with honors from George Washington University in 1946, beaming Harry Truman, President of the United States, clad in cap and gown, presented her with her diploma.

Meanwhile, Bess Truman wanted nothing more than to return to Independence at the end of Harry Truman's presidential term. She fervently hoped he would not run for election in 1948. None of the political experts thought he could win the election, but Harry Truman was determined.

Then began one of the strangest campaign tours in history—a rugged fight against seemingly impossible odds. Newspapers, magazines, and public opinion polls said he didn't have a chance. He, Bess, and Margaret rode the "doomed" campaign train thousands of miles up and down and across the nation.

At every whistle stop, as soon as he finished his hard-hitting speech from the back platform of the train, he would suddenly grin and call out, "How'ja like to meet The Boss?"; then quickly turn, reach for Bess Truman's hand, and draw her out from the car. As she smiled and waved, Harry would again grin, saying, "And now meet The Boss's Boss," as he introduced Margaret. She joined her mother, laughing and waving, while Harry beamed at them both and at the people. As the train pulled out, all three kept waving and smiling from the platform.

It was exhausting work, especially for Bess, who disliked

any form of familiarity, but Harry Truman needed her help in reaching out to the public—getting people to vote for him. The strenuous grind succeeded.

On November 2, 1948, in one of the greatest upsets in the nation's history, Harry Truman was elected and returned to the office of President of the United States. Another four years of duty for Bess.

Within a few days of their return to the White House, they had to move. Engineers had inspected the 148-year-old White House and found it unsafe. Parts of the mansion were sagging and crumbling with age. Congress appropriated some $5,575,000 to reconstruct it. While the White House was being rebuilt, the Trumans lived in Blair House. This handsome home, built about 1824, stood at 1651 Pennsylvania Avenue, across from the White House. In 1942 the United States government had bought Blair House to accommodate distinguished visitors.

While the Trumans were still living in Blair House, Bess went through some of the most terrifying hours of her life. Shortly after lunch on November 5, 1950, President Truman went to his room to take a short nap before speaking at a dedicatory ceremony. He had scarcely fallen asleep when gunshots burst at the door of Blair House. Two Puerto Rican revolutionaries were trying to shoot their way into Blair House to kill the President of the United States. They were fought off by the President's special guards, one of whom was killed and another seriously wounded. Harry Truman, however, quietly insisted on going out to keep his dedicatory appointment at Arlington Cemetery.

Those shots thundered in Bess Truman's memory long after others forgot. In the history of the United States, assassins had managed to kill three Presidents—Abraham

Lincoln, James Garfield, William McKinley. Twice, assassins had tried and mercifully failed—Franklin Delano Roosevelt, President-elect, and Harry S Truman, thirty-third President . . . and Bess's husband. And there were at least two more years of risk.

But Bess Truman was, as her husband said more than once, "a good soldier." She hid her personal concern and matched the President's own strong, confident attitude of "We have a job to do."

Through the next year American voters wondered if Harry Truman would run for re-election as President in 1952. On the evening of March 29, 1952, he and Bess Truman attended the Democratic party's annual banquet in memory of Andrew Jackson, seventh President of the United States. Principal speaker of the evening, Harry Truman spoke steadily for several minutes, then looked up from the pages before him and paused—just long enough to catch the attention of everyone there and the thousands listening. Then, almost flatly, came Harry Truman's familiar voice, "I shall not be a candidate for reelection."

Broadcast listeners could hear in the banquet hall cries of "Oh, no! You have to!" He only smiled his thanks and deliberately resumed his prepared speech. As he left the banquet hall with Bess, camera shots showed her erect, smartly dressed, Harry's arm through hers. She was relieved and happy. She knew the burden he had carried—the fateful decisions he had been forced to make in his seven years as President, including the use of the first atom bomb and construction of the first hydrogen bomb. In a few months Harry Truman would be relieved of that burden.

Mamie Doud Eisenhower

(1896)

IT was the summer of 1952. Mamie Eisenhower had come
to an important decision—to make all the campaign appearances she could with her soldier-husband, General
Dwight D. Eisenhower, who was the Republican candidate
for president. The decision was not easy for Mamie. Until
then she had resolutely stayed out of public life as much as
possible. In all their thirty-six years of marriage her only
ambition was to make a comfortable home for her husband,
"Ike" Eisenhower.

The decision to campaign with him meant facing the
stares of inquisitive crowds hour after hour, day after day—
in gaunt auditoriums; in blaring parades and rallies; in
muddy farm fields; on open balconies; and on the windy
rear platform of the campaign train at every whistle stop—
and trying to look pleasant every moment. Few experiences
could be more exhausting to a beginner; and, for years,
Mamie had been suffering a slight heart condition and had
had to conserve her strength.

When General Eisenhower began his tour early in September, he was already world-famous. His nickname stood
boldly in headlines of newspapers here and abroad. In

photographs, newsreels, and on television, his strong face and wide grin were instantly recognized by millions of people. Wherever he went, crowds shouted, "I like Ike!"

Mamie was virtually unknown and completely without experience in politics. Some Republicans even feared that she might handicap Ike through her lack of political "know-how."

They need not have worried. Mamie had two splendid resources. She had the discretion of a good "army wife" and, equally important, she had a gift for just being herself. Only five feet three inches, she was an engagingly small figure beside her broad-shouldered husband. As the crowds stared curiously at her, she greeted them with her quick smile. In some way, just by her expression and a wave of her hand, Mamie let them all know that she was friendly and wanted them to be friends with her. People everywhere grinned and waved back, and felt as though they had known her for years.

Within the first few days of the campaign she became an important person in Ike's drive for votes. Men and women still shouted, "I like Ike!" And to that slogan they now added, "We like Mamie!" A veteran newspaper reporter declared, "Mamie must be worth at least 50 electoral votes to Ike!"

The delighted public was discovering what Mamie's close friends had always known—she was an unspoiled person with an enthusiastic ability to adapt to unexpected situations and to all kinds of people. After reporters had approached her several times in Washington during World War II and asked, "What's new today, Mrs. Eisenhower?" she grinned and answered, "Don't keep calling me Mrs. Eisenhower. Just call me Mamie—it's more friendly."

Mamie was born November 14, 1896, in Boone, Iowa. She was of English and Swedish descent. Her father was John Sheldon Doud. He met young Elivera Mathilda Carlson, and when Elivera was only sixteen years old she married John Doud. Their second of four daughters was Mamie —Mamie Geneva Doud. Before Mamie was a year old the family moved to Cedar Rapids, Iowa; then, when she was six, to Pueblo, Colorado, and later to Colorado Springs. In 1905, when Mamie was nine, the family packed up again and moved to Denver, Colorado, where Mamie grew up.

Her father was so successful in the meat packing business that he retired in 1907 when only thirty-six years old. As a prosperous man, he was able to give his four daughters many advantages. He bought a comfortable eleven-room brick house at 750 Lafayette Street in the fashionable section of east Denver.

The four lively Doud girls—Mamie, Eleanor, "Buster," and "Mike"—soon made it the headquarters for the whole neighborhood. Boys and girls gathered on the porch for cookies, grape juice, and fudge, or flocked to the piano while Mamie played by ear and sang the hits of the day.

Mr. Doud was devoted to his wife and daughters. As an indulgent father, he was happy to let Mamie choose the decorations for her own room. She selected white wallpaper striped in pink roses, with light green draperies, and green carpet. These remained her favorite colors all through her life, appearing in every home she made—"Mamie's trademark."

In the autumn of 1915 the Doud family, as it had done for many years, left Denver to spend the winter in a southern climate. They took a house in San Antonio, Texas. One fine October day the Douds drove out to Fort Sam Houston

to visit friends. There Mamie met a young second lieutenant just graduated from West Point.

Lieutenant Dwight David Eisenhower, age twenty-five,
took an admiring look at young Mamie Doud, almost nineteen. He saw a slender, blue-eyed girl, in the stylish ankle-
length costume of the day. A white chip sailor hat tilted
over her brown hair.

Lieutenant Eisenhower soon became "Ike" to Mamie,
and he courted her with unyielding persistence. The determined young second lieutenant won. On February 14,
1916, they became engaged. As an engagement ring, he
gave her a replica of his West Point class ring, amethyst
set in gold.

The young couple was married July 1, 1916, at high noon
in the Doud home in Denver. They stood before the fireplace, the mantel banked in pink gladioli. At one side, a
harpist played their wedding music. Mamie's wedding dress
was Chantilly lace. Her groom, who had been promoted to
first lieutenant that day, wore his dress whites.

Marriage to a young army officer launched Mamie into
a very different kind of life. From a comfortable home she
went to live in a two-room apartment in the officers' quarters at Fort Sam Houston—on Lieutenant Eisenhower's
scanty pay of $161.67 per month.

Mamie never became a great success as a cook. After
many meals in the officers' mess, which they could scarcely
afford, Lieutenant Eisenhower decided to learn to cook.
Eventually he became as celebrated for his cooking as
Mamie wasn't.

Mamie, however, learned other important things in her
new life. When she married, her father had said, "Live
within your husband's income." She learned through neces-

sity how to manage their income, and took charge of the family finances. In later years she said, "There may have been times when we had only a dollar in the bank, but we have never owed a cent in our lives."

She also learned how to be a good "army wife." In the closely knit life of an army post, an officer's wife must get along easily with people of many different temperaments, avoid cliques, keep out of controversies, and keep secrets. She must also move without complaint when her husband is ordered to a new post. Above all, she must make a comfortable home for her family, no matter where they are stationed.

Little more than a year after she was married, Mamie learned one of the hardest things about being a service wife —meeting loneliness when her husband's duty separated him from her. Four days before their first child was born, Lieutenant Eisenhower was ordered to Fort Oglethorpe, Georgia. In Texas, at Fort Sam Houston, on September 24, 1917, Mamie Eisenhower gave birth to a son, Doud Dwight Eisenhower. He died of scarlet fever in 1921. Their second and last child, John Sheldon Doud Eisenhower, was born in Denver in 1922.

During World War I, while Ike fretted at stateside assignments, the Eisenhowers were stationed at Fort Meade, Maryland, and later Camp Colt, near Gettysburg, Pennsylvania.

Then came a series of moves that tested Mamie. With some twenty-five moves in thirty-six years—by ship, by train, by army truck—they couldn't carry much of their own furniture around with them. And, if they could, there would be very little left of it after the first few loadings and unloadings. Mamie, however, brought a feeling of home to every new post. She insisted on taking their own rugs, pictures, family photographs, music, and records, and Ike's awards and mementos. Through all her various moves she carried samples of the beloved pink and greens which had brightened her girlhood room in Denver. On every new post, she did her own room in pink and green.

The living room was always a sunny yellow. When she was decorating her first army house, a friend told her: "Mamie, you can't beat God's sunshine. No matter how dull the day, yellow will bring cheerfulness into the home."

Those moves carried the Eisenhowers halfway around the world. They lived in the Panama Canal Zone, the Philippines, Europe, and in army posts in every part of the United States. Some of their settings were not pleasant. Of their home in the Canal Zone in 1922–24, a house on stilts, Mamie later recalled: "There were bats all over the place, and every manner of crawling thing."

In 1936, when John was fourteen, they joined Ike in the Philippines, where they stayed four years. Their return to the United States in 1940 delighted her; but she was not prepared for the swift change that lay just ahead. As the threat of war mounted, Lieutenant Colonel Eisenhower received swift promotion. In June 1942, only seven months after the United States entered World War II, Eisenhower, as a major general, was put in command of all American forces in the British Isles.

He left in June to take up his command in England. From then until after the end of the savage war in August 1945, Mamie lived in loneliness and unceasing anxiety for Ike's safety. She went to almost no public places, fearing people might recognize her and think her indifferent to the dangers besetting their own husbands and sons.

She wrote to General Eisenhower every day, and was delighted when his letters contained requests for little personal articles. Her happiest times were slipping quietly out to buy him "drug store grass slippers," records of ballads, and all the Westerns she could find. Red Cross work helped to fill the lonely gap.

In June 1944, Mamie went to West Point to see her son John graduate from the Military Academy. The graduation was on June 6—D-Day, the day Eisenhower's Allied forces launched the invasion of Europe.

The triumphal end of World War II in 1945 made General of the Army Eisenhower one of the most famous men in the world. Despite his high position, Mamie determinedly remained in the background.

Their long army life seemed to come to an end in 1948, when General Eisenhower resigned from the service to become president of Columbia University in New York City. Mamie and he moved—another move, even as civilians!—to the university president's mansion at 60 Morningside Drive in New York.

They had not been long at Columbia when Mamie developed a happy new "hobby." She delighted to baby-sit with her first grandchild, Dwight David Eisenhower II, born at West Point, March 31, 1948. When the second grandchild, Barbara Anne, was born in 1949, Mamie fixed up a nursery in the mansion so the young Eisenhowers could bring the babies from West Point as often as possible.

At fifty-three, Mamie was looking forward to a comfortable "civilian old age." General Eisenhower and she even bought a home—their first own home. It was an 189-acre farm at Gettysburg, Pennsylvania. Mamie planned how she would remodel and decorate the old farmhouse. While Ike was president of Columbia they would use it as a vacation retreat; then, when he retired from public life, they would make it their permanent home.

Little more than a year after they bought their Gettysburg home, in which they had not yet lived, she was packing up again to live in France. She was again an army wife. General Eisenhower had been called back into service to be commander of SHAPE—Supreme Headquarters, Allied Powers in Europe.

On the voyage the General relaxed with his painting. He was a self-taught amateur. Mamie "sat" for him. Once a friend studied an oil portrait the General had done of Mamie, and remonstrated that it looked stiff. Mamie grinned and explained, "Oh, that isn't Ike's fault. I just didn't talk while he was painting, and so I don't look natural. I'm always talking."

In France they stayed at a hotel in Versailles while Mamie inspected several houses selected by the French government for them. Most of them were too pretentious for her. She chose the Villa St. Pierre near the tiny village of Marnes-la-Coquette, about a half-hour's drive from Paris. Fourteen leading French interior decorators then "did" the villa, but Mamie gave it her home touch by quietly insisting that the living room be sunny yellow, her room pink and green, and the family photographs be given prominent places where she and the General could enjoy them.

In 1951 pressure was renewed on the General to run for the Republican nomination. At last, he decided that it was his duty to seek the nomination. Once again Mamie packed up. Flying in the General's plane, the *Columbine*—named for the state flower of Mamie's Colorado—they landed in Washington on June 1, 1952.

General Eisenhower began his campaign at once, with Mamie at his side. On June 4 they journeyed to Abilene, Kansas, the General's boyhood home. They clambered down from their streamliner into an open field, where hundreds awaited them. There the General and three of his brothers set the cornerstone for an Eisenhower Foundation Museum.

After driving into the city of Abilene, the General and Mamie climbed out on the marquee of the Sunflower Hotel to review a parade in their honor. As the floats passed by, spectators saw the General grin when he sighted the "marriage float" representing "Mamie and Ike" as bride and groom. He suddenly turned and hugged Mamie.

Later that day when the General set out to shake hands with the men of Abilene, Mamie suggested: "Tell the girls —I mean the ladies—to come back here, and I'll talk to them." Mamie was already in the swing of making new friends for Ike.

Back in her hometown of Denver for a brief rest, Mamie took a woman reporter on a tour of her girlhood sights— even the iron hitching post where her father had tied their mare, "old Kate." As Mamie and the reporter started on their rounds, several youngsters called out, "Hiya, Mamie!" Waving, Mamie grinned and said, "Hiya, kids!" Mamie was still Mamie Doud of Denver, friend of all the neighborhood.

When the Republican convention met in Chicago in July, Mamie again retired to the background. She spent most of her time in her room at the Blackstone Hotel, watching the convention on television and greeting delegates' wives. Behind the scenes she was going after "votes for Ike" in her own way.

Early in the afternoon of July 11, he won the nomination on the first ballot. A few weeks later Mamie and he launched their strenuous campaign tour—the tour that soon had the crowds shouting, "We like Mamie!"

On November 4, 1952, he was overwhelmingly elected thirty-fourth President of the United States.

Until the inauguration in January their home was the Columbia University mansion on Morningside Drive. There, late in November, Mamie became an amateur actress. That is, she skillfully entered the necessary "conspiracy" to keep the whereabouts of President-elect Eisenhower a secret. During his campaign he had pledged himself to visit Korea in an effort to halt the fighting. The utmost secrecy had to be kept to guard his safety en route.

His departure was like melodrama. At 5:30 in the morning of November 29, while most of New York was still asleep, the General and a secret service man slipped out of the mansion and sped to the airport. For the next few days Mamie blandly followed her routine, never indicating in any way that the General was absent. To help draw attention away from the mansion, she made a well-publicized trip to Washington to inspect the newly renovated White House with Mrs. Truman as hostess.

On January 20, 1953, the General was inaugurated President of the United States. Near him, at his right, on the special platform in front of the Capitol, was Mamie. Her eyes never left his face as he put his hand on the Bible and spoke the grave, resounding words of the oath of office: "I, Dwight D. Eisenhower, do solemnly swear that I will faithfully execute the Office of President of the United States, and will to the best of my ability preserve, protect, and defend the Constitution of the United States."

When he finished, Mamie looked as though she were fighting back tears at the enormous responsibility he had assumed. But the new President turned from the microphone and smiled at her. Then he quickly walked to her and took her in his arms.

Returning to the microphone to give his inaugural address, he paused a moment for silence. He then created an innovation—before beginning his speech, he offered a prayer he had written only a few hours earlier: "Almighty God . . . give us, we pray, the power to discern clearly right from wrong, and allow all our words and actions to be governed thereby and by the laws of this land. Especially we pray that our concern shall be for all the people regardless of station, race, or calling."

That evening at the two inaugural balls, Mamie wore a full-skirted Renoir pink gown of *peau de soie*. The sleeveless, V-necked gown sparkled with pink and rose stones. Her gloves, shoes, and evening bag—encrusted with 3,456 pink stones, beads, and pink pearls—were of matching fabric. Her necklace, earrings, and bracelet were specially made costume jewelry—artificial pearls linked with rhinestones. Later, she gave her costume, as is the custom, for display in the Smithsonian Institution in Washington.

The White House was now their home—or, rather, residence, for there is little that is homelike in most of the vast, formal White House where every year about one million sightseers troop through the main floor rooms. Undaunted, Mamie converted her bedroom on the second floor into pink and light green, with restful green walls.

Like so many women before her, Mamie soon learned that being First Lady is not only a fulltime job but also a most exacting one. Her correspondence alone consumed hours even with the help of secretaries, for she received some three hundred to seven hundred letters a day. Every day brought receptions or teas or dedication ceremonies or public tours or visits to charitable institutions, and wherever she went she had to shake hands. In the White House, she shook the hands of some sixteen thousand official visitors in just her first "season"—January to June of 1953.

It was not the comfortable homey "middle age" she had dreamed of; but, as long as she could help Ike in any way, she would put all her heart into it. As she said just before going into the White House as First Lady: "All through our married life, things like this have happened to test our strength. . . . I've seen our life together shaped by unexpected turns, utterly beyond human conception, and I begin to think there is a divine plan back of it all and that Ike is part of it. He's really a great man. I'm thankful for the privilege of being by his side."

Further Reading

MARTHA (DANDRIDGE) CUSTIS WASHINGTON. *Martha Washington, Our First Lady,* by Alice Curtis Desmond (Dodd, 1942). *Story of Martha Washington,* by Jeannette C. Nolan (Grosset, 1954). *Washington's Lady: The Life of Martha Washington,* by Elswyth Thane (Duell—Meredith, 1960). *Martha, Daughter of Virginia,* by Marguerite Vance (Dutton, 1947).

ABIGAIL SMITH ADAMS. *Abigail Adams: Leading Lady,* by Mildred Criss (Dodd, 1952). *Abigail Adams: The President's Lady,* by Regina Z. Kelly (Houghton, 1962). *Abigail Adams: A Girl of Colonial Days,* by Jean Brown Wagoner (Bobbs, 1949).

MARTHA JEFFERSON RANDOLPH *and* MARIA JEFFERSON EPPES. *Thomas Jefferson, His Many Talents,* by Johanna Johnston (Dodd, 1961). *Thomas Jefferson,* by Manuel Komroff (Messner, 1961). *Thomas Jefferson and His World,* by Henry Moscow and Dumas Malone (American Heritage—Meredith, 1960). *Domestic Life of Thomas Jefferson,* by Sarah N. Randolph (Ungar, 1958).

DOROTHEA (PAYNE) TODD MADISON. *Glamorous Dolly Madison,* by Alice Curtis Desmond (Dodd, 1946). *Dolly Madison,* by Jane Mayer (Random House, 1954). *Dolly Madison: Quaker Girl*, by Helen Albee Monsell (Bobbs, 1953). *Dolley Madison*, by Jeannette C. Nolan (Messner, 1958).

ELIZABETH KORTRIGHT MONROE. *Autobiography of James Monroe*, edited by Stuart Gerry Brown (Syracuse, 1959). *James Monroe*, by William Penn Cresson (University of North Carolina, 1946).

LOUISA JOHNSON ADAMS. *John Quincy Adams: The Critical Years*, by Robert A. East (Twayne, 1962).

RACHEL (DONELSON) ROBARDS JACKSON. *Real Book About Andrew Jackson*, by Harold Coy (Doubleday, 1952). *Rachel Jackson: Tennessee Girl*, by Christine Govan (Bobbs, 1955). *Andrew Jackson*, by Clara Judson (Follett, 1954). *The Jacksons of Tennessee*, by Marguerite Vance (Dutton, 1953).

ANNA SYMMES HARRISON. *Tippecanoe and Tyler, Too!* Stanley Young (Random House, 1957).

MARY TODD LINCOLN. *Abraham Lincoln's World*, by Genevieve Foster (Scribner, 1944). *Abraham Lincoln*, by Manuel Komroff (Putnam, 1959). *I Mary: A Biography of the Girl Who Married Abraham Lincoln*, by Ruth Painter Randall (Little, 1959). *Mary Lincoln: Wife and Widow*, by Carl Sandburg (Harcourt, Brace, 1932). *Mary Todd Lincoln: Girl of the Bluegrass*, by Katharine E. Wilkie (Bobbs, 1954).

ELIZA McCARDLE JOHNSON *and* MARTHA JOHNSON PATTERSON. *Tragic Era: The Revolution After Lincoln*, by Claude G. Bowers (Houghton, 1929). *Defender of the Constitution: Andrew Johnson*, by Margaret Green (Messner, 1962). *Andy Johnson: The Tailor Who Became President*, by Milton Lomask (Farrar, Straus, 1962).

JULIA DENT GRANT. *Mr. Lincoln's General: Ulysses S. Grant*, by Roy Meredith (Dutton, 1959). *General's Wife*, by Ishbel

Ross (Dodd, 1959). *Ulysses S. Grant,* by Henry Thomas (Putnam, 1961).

FRANCES FOLSOM CLEVELAND. *Grover Cleveland,* by Edwin P. Hoyt (Reilly & Lee).

IDA SAXTON McKINLEY. *In the Days of McKinley,* by Margaret Kernochan Leech (Harper, 1959).

EDITH CAROW ROOSEVELT, *Adventure in Courage: The Story of Theodore Roosevelt,* by Frances Cavanah (Rand McNally, 1961). *The Roosevelt Family of Sagamore Hill,* by Hermann Hagedorn (Macmillan, 1954). *Theodore Roosevelt,* by Clara I. Judson (Follett, 1953). *Day Before Yesterday: The Reminiscences of Mrs. Theodore Roosevelt, Jr.,* by Mrs. Theodore Roosevelt, Jr. (Doubleday, 1959).

ELLEN AXSON WILSON *and* EDITH (BOLLING) GALT WILSON. *Woodrow Wilson: An Intimate Memoir,* by Cary T. Grayson (Holt, Rinehart & Winston, 1960). *Edith Bolling Wilson,* by Alden Hatch (Dodd, 1961). *Woodrow Wilson: A Biography for Young People,* by Alden Hatch (Holt, Rinehart & Winston, 1947). *Woodrow Wilson,* by Alfred Steinberg (Putnam, 1961).

GRACE GOODHUE COOLIDGE. *Meet Calvin Coolidge,* edited by Edward C. Lathem (Greene). *Grace Coolidge and Her Era,* by Ishbel Ross (Dodd, 1962).

LOU HENRY HOOVER. *Herbert Hoover: American Quaker,* by David Hinshaw (Farrar, Straus, 1950). *Herbert Hoover: Engineer, Humanitarian and Statesman,* by Dorothy H. McGee (Dodd, 1959).

ELEANOR ROOSEVELT. *Story of Eleanor Roosevelt,* by Jeanette Eaton (Morrow, 1956). *The Eleanor Roosevelt We Remember,* by Helen Gahagan Douglas (Hill and Wang, 1963). *Story of Eleanor Roosevelt,* by Lorena Hickok (Grosset, 1959).

F. D. R.: A Pictorial Biography, by Stefan Lorant (Simon and Schuster, 1950). *Autobiography*, by Eleanor Roosevelt (Harper, 1961). *Eleanor Roosevelt*, by Alfred Steinberg (Putnam, 1959).

BESS WALLACE TRUMAN. *White House Sailor*, by William M. Rigdon and James Derieux (Doubleday).

MAMIE DOUD EISENHOWER. *Eisenhower, Captive Hero*, by Marquis W. Childs (Harcourt, 1958). *Eisenhower: The Inside Story*, by Robert J. Donovan (Harper, 1956). *Ike Eisenhower: Statesman and Soldier of Peace*, by Delos W. Lovelace (Crowell, 1961).

JACQUELINE BOUVIER KENNEDY. *First Lady*, by Charlotte Curtis (Pyramid, 1962). *Portrait: The Emergence of John F. Kennedy*, by Jacques Lowe (McGraw, 1961). *Jacqueline Bouvier Kennedy*, by Mary van Rensselaer Thayer (Doubleday, 1961). *A Tour of the White House with Mrs. John F. Kennedy*, by Perry Wolff (Doubleday, 1962; also Dell, 1963).

The chapter concerning Mrs. Kennedy was checked by her personal secretary at the White House.

GENERAL. *Presidents in American History*, by Charles A. Beard (Messner, 1961). *Meet the Presidents*, by Frances Cavanah and Elizabeth L. Crandall (Macrae Smith, 1962). *Thirty-four Roads to the White House*, by Alberta P. Graham (Nelson, 1957). *Ladies of the White House*, by Logan B. Logan (Vantage, 1962). *Our First Ladies: From Martha Washington to Jacqueline Kennedy*, by Jane and Burt McConnell (Crowell, 1961). *America and Its Presidents*, by Earl S. Miers (Grosset, 1959). *Know Your Presidents and Their Wives*, by George E. Ross (Rand McNally, 1961). *Famous Women of America*, by William Oliver Stevens (Dodd, 1950).

Index